By Time is Everything Revealed

And Other Irish Proverbs for Mindful Living

Fiann Ó Nualláin

GILL BOOKS

Gill Books
Hume Avenue
Park West
Dublin 12
www.gillbooks.ie

Gill Books is an imprint of M.H. Gill and Co.

© Fiann Ó Nualláin 2017

978 07171 7098 2

Designed by Jen Patton

Printed by CPI Group (UK) Ltd, Croydon, CRO 4YY

This book is typeset in Lato and Fontin.

The paper used in this book comes from the wood pulp of managed forests. For every tree felled, at least one tree is planted, thereby renewing natural resources.

A CIP catalogue record for this book is available from the British Library.

5 4 3

Thanks to Brother Hurley for the martial arts flicks; to Sensei Jimmy for the martial arts tricks and discipline; to Teresa Hanaway for opening the door to spiritual exercises; to my aunties Laurie, Alice and Rita for always having a turn of phrase or a proverb on the go; to the proverb collators from Cormac Mac Airt to Micheál Ó Longáin, the Irish Folklore Commission and Laurence Flanagan; to Lisa Kelly for her counsel and care; and finally, a special thanks to Sarah Liddy and Sheila Armstrong for chiselling my often esoteric ramblings into this very readable book.

Contents

Introduction

P roverbs exist in every culture. They capture wisdom and set guidelines for each society's paradigms. They frame the lived and shared experience of a culture's people, speaking of the collective consciousness and also to the single individual seeking awareness or wisdom. Many have come down through the generations to educate and edify each new generation. Within Irish culture they are prized so much that there is even a proverb about proverbs – *ní féidir an seanfhocal a shárú* – a proverb cannot be refuted. At this point, you may think that remains to be seen, but by the conclusion of this book you may have a new understanding, along with a set of tools to cultivate mindfulness, psychological wellbeing and spiritual awareness.

Mindfulness, psychological wellbeing and spiritual awareness are really the same thing. They are all a means and an end, and they are each a solace and a catalyst in life. Think of it like this: a river is water, a glacier is water and rain is also water. You may perceive and interact with each one differently, but they are all water nonetheless. So you may engage with mindfulness to find yourself or to find God; you may use it to break negative thought patterns or energise your self-worth – it still comes with the potential to secure those other possibilities too. The thawing glacier becomes a river and the river may evaporate to become rain. Mindfulness is you knowing that you are water, and being aware that today – or in this now – you are also a river, rain or glacier. Mindfulness is feeling the solidity of the glacier and not denying your potential to be a stream. Mindfulness is not fretting over being rain or stream – you are water, ever moving and multifaceted. Mindfulness is experiencing life, and, through that experiencing, manifesting both psychological wellbeing and spiritual awareness.

Mindfulness is often described as 'now' – as the ultimate present – but nothing in life is so easy. Yes, you can and will master the switch to 'fully present and in control', but that's not an instantly acquired skill. Some work and a little time is required. Before we can *be*, we must first *become*.

This is a book about becoming, but there is also a measure of doing. You may find stillness in the meditations and peace through mindful living, but you will also find dynamism. Action is as spiritually and psychologically potent as quiet rectitude. The actions and exercises in this book are catalysts to transformation – just as the proverbs and my thoughts on their meanings are prompts to becoming more mindful.

Mindfulness and the other techniques that I weave throughout this book – positive psychology, cognitive behavioural therapy and awareness activation – are not mastered in a moment. The title of this book makes that clear – *by time is everything revealed*. Time is involved, as we must build up skills and rewire the brain. But soon enough, the effort and time we apply will yield awareness and a mindful self – everything will be revealed. If you take the time, then there is potential to apply the content as a method or course, to achieve a more integrated mindful experience and to develop some sustainable practises that will benefit you over the rest of your life. I use fifty-two dedicated proverbs as motivational jump-off points for mindful reflections, actions and exercises throughout the book.

The Irish language word for a proverb is a *seanfhocail*. A *seanfhocal* means an old word, but these old words are not just 'sayings': they possess a gravitas that has been carried down through time. Some are uniquely Irish – indigenous sayings that speak volumes about the Irish psyche – and some are manifestations of biblical proverbs, English idioms or the paradigms of a particular epoch. They are not passed on as cultural curiosities, out of historical interest or even out of nostalgia – they are relevant in each generation and survive on their own merits by the power of their proverbial wisdom and connection.

When I sat down to write this book, the phrase 'old words for new ears' struck me. During the writing process, the 'new ears' signified not just the modern world, not just the uninitiated or first-time participant. The 'new ears' were also symbolic – to hear afresh, to hear with newness – to come to the seanfhocail as more than an old saying but as a living voice for here and now.

In mindfulness we experience the now. In Christianity you are invited to be renewed, in Buddhism you awaken and become. Each of these and other faiths and systems ask participants to listen to and hear a message in order to experience a transformation. Some of you will know these proverbs well, some of you will be new ears. Either way, I hope that in their new context as lessons of mindfulness, the transforming spirit of these old words will renew, refresh and reinvigorate. Let nothing refute that either.

My personal path to mindfulness

I was the sort of kid who wanted to be the Indian and not the cowboy (even before I empathised politically and spiritually with that side). I didn't care much for cops and robbers and really would rather have been off inhabiting the persona of Cú Chulainn (one of the greatest Irish heroes from our mythos) or Bruce Lee (whose philosophy would soon impress me as much as his cinematic martial arts). Maybe both of those figures were shaped by a self-perception as an outsider warrior, which necessitated dignity, respect for others, honed skills and discipline. So the *play* scenarios of my formative years were as much about feeling the power and honing it as asserting power itself. Self-control and self-confidence came when I joined a karate club aged eight. I joined with several school friends and I was perhaps seeking to perfect my inner Bruce Lee, if not my command of martial arts. My school would show martial arts and action hero movies on Fridays as an ongoing fundraiser, and that sparked in us a desire for these action hero skills.

The karate would eventually bring me into direct contact with the difference between being 'mind full' (inner dialogue and the noise of unfocused thoughts) and having or adopting 'in the moment clarity' – that which we now call mindfulness. Clearing your mind before a bout, being super alert to the reality of your opponent and focusing attention on their body language and movement patterns meant you could defeat them more quickly, without bruises or humiliation. Decisiveness kept everybody's honour intact. You respected your opponent, so ego was not a factor, and being mindful in the ring was as important as your physical moves. So over the next few years and into my early teens, being mindful in the ring taught me to be mindful in life beyond the ring. And so it came to be that *faghann iarraidh iarraidh eile* – the seeking for one thing finds another.

That's not even hindsight – that is just how it happened. Events follow events, decisions beget other decisions, life experience leads to more life experience. Picking up this book is perhaps a start, but there is a next step. In fact, picking up this book may be the next step in something that began much earlier. Not everything is linear, and not everything is so apparent. I joined karate to jump around and kick, but it kicked me in the eye with insights into something else. There are so many things that happen in life that lead to a different place than expected. I am sure there is a science behind why people pick up one hobby or interest over another, and I am sure there is a debate as to whether it's because you were wired for it (physical aptitude or mental aptitude) or it wired you (the interest in sports made you fitter and so healthier, or the chess made you good at your eventual business career). Whatever the case, we know mindfulness can rewire you – adjust your thought patterns and the thought-to-feeling relationship – and so control your mood and reactions. We know it can condition your stress reactions and provide self-control and movement out of negativity and ruts.

The karate could have led to me being a sportsperson, but it led somewhere else instead. What I do know is that no experience is wasted. It is all part of the fabric of life, and some experiences may result in rewards years later. We can also use mindfulness to alter our reactions and move beyond the experiences that may affect us in less than positive ways, freeing ourselves from limitations on our full potential.

Looking back, I guess I first encountered mindfulness at quite an early age. It was not yet the globally embraced tool it is today, and it was not even called mindfulness at that time. Between the ages of eight and fourteen it was showing itself to me as I was engaging with it as a martial arts discipline, as a device to get in the zone and out of bouts unharmed. It was not to the front of my brain as a natural part of my everyday experience of life, let alone a spiritual technique or a physiological tool to calm my issues or get through bouts of depression. I had suffered from periods of despondency and depression from early childhood and in keeping with everything else I had experienced spiritual crises early on too – all of which I now see as the mud and sediment required to root the lotus. It would take its time to grow and unfold but the negative experiences did not rot the bud – they just made it flower more beautifully. I was in my twenties before I came to this realisation – *tá fáth le gach nidh* – there is a reason for everything. I am grateful to depression for teaching me resilience, independence and compassion. Nothing in life is wasted.

By my early teens, I had read a couple of books by Bruce Lee and also Morihei Ueshiba (the founder of aikido), I had begun to read Sun Tzu, Lao Tzu and Confucius and I was leaning more into the spiritual side of things. Simultaneously, I had become a vegetarian, more respectful of nature, and had encountered the Krishna consciousness with the Hare Krishna community in Dublin. The martial arts had led to personal discipline, which had led to meditation, and that led to reading more about Zen and other Buddhist philosophies, which had led to exploring the tenets of all religions and a search for more insight. *Sati* – as 'mindfulness' was called – and *satori* (self-awareness) were just around the corner. I was at that point in life where everything seems to be happening: spiritual yearnings, sexual yearnings, the call to be individual but also to belong. At that age, the big questions arise. Who am I? What am I? Why am I? And at that time I personally didn't find satisfactory

11

answers to those conundrums within the Catholic tradition in which I had been raised – so it was easy for me to drop it and look to other faiths and their texts and systems to get a different perspective. When I wasn't listening to music or thinking about the girl down the road, I read everything I could get my hands on about religion, philosophy and psychology. I had a thirst for knowledge and an interest in the human condition and the divine experience. Eventually, I found the translations of Thomas Cleary and began to really explore Buddhism. All of a sudden, 'Who am I?' was replaced with 'What is *mu*?' and spiritual and metaphysical conundrums became *koans* for a time.

That is not to say I became a Buddhist, or a Hare Krishna, or a born again anything. I became both faithful and faithless – I felt I didn't need a religious structure to define my spiritual self or my self-expression and I soon realised that the questions 'Who am I?' and 'What is *mu*?' didn't matter – the answer was the same: everything and nothing. I acknowledged that the giving of attention to those sorts of questions could bring about a portion or invocation of *sati/* mindfulness – that the activated mind in the moment of the question, in the moment of the pondering, in the moment of realisations or non-realisations, was, in that instance or 'now', of absolute purity and unity. It was, in that moment, utterly connected to everything that is everything and all that is nothing. And therein is *satori* – comprehension and understanding. But once that hit me, I didn't need to keep asking. I wasn't searching any more, I was just enjoying looking further – or, perhaps I should say, just looking more.

By my late teens and early twenties I could again look at and gain great joy from the works of writers in the Christian tradition such as Thomas Keating and Anthony de Mello – exploring parables, a system I knew well from my first fourteen years on the planet. For the first time, I saw a message that I had missed in the faith of my parents – 'the Kingdom of God is within and all around'. I could live the rest of my life in the Kingdom of God. Life was the Kingdom of God. Prayer was the Kingdom, drinking was the Kingdom, chasing girls was the Kingdom, fasting, feasting, running, sitting still, whatever I did was the Kingdom – the Kingdom was mindful living. *Being* was and is the Kingdom.

Sometimes you forget that every second of your life is the Kingdom of God, and other times you bubble up with the joy of it. For the most part, life goes on – as the saying goes, 'before I was enlightened I chopped wood and carried water, after enlightenment I chopped wood and carried water'. Enlightenment/ mindfulness is a superpower, but you won't get a cape and the ability to fly or stop bullets. You will remain human – mindfully human – and human fully. The firewood won't chop itself, and if it did, you would miss out on chopping it mindfully. I move in and out of the moment, in and out of grace, in and out of depression and in and out of palpable joy. That's life. That's even a good life. Mindfulness has made my lows more bearable and less frequent. It has made my pleasures and highs all the more of an experience – because I am with them as they happen. I am living my life. So many people just daydream their life. To me, it doesn't matter if you only live once or are eternally reincarnated – live your life or live your lives – but live. Experience it. Life can be cruel, heart-breaking sometimes, but also beautiful and joyous. Live the low, live the high, know you have lived.

I have a background in holistic therapy and have spent a large portion of my working life delivering workshops, clinics, courses and programmes in the therapeutic use of both horticulture and art, incorporating the dynamics of holistic practices to heal the whole person and not just the condition, to form social cohesion and not just paint over a graffiti wall or create a community garden on waste ground. I have worked with children at risk, adults in recovery, self-help groups, corporate and state bodies. So mindfulness has not just helped me personally, it has also been invaluable to me professionally. It was a professional context that led me to first use seanfhocail as a trigger device to open debate or tempt enquiry. I was creating a garden with a dementia group, and the old sayings and songs were great motivational tools to keep the group in good morale and encourage active participation. Later, I worked with some early school leavers on a community park project and we researched the local history to find an appropriate theme and design. Part of that included taking oral history from within the community (to make it an intergenerational project) and here the old sayings broke some barriers and made it fun.

Those experiences sowed the seeds for this book – to cultivate positivity through interaction with culture. With some groups and clients, the art project or the gardening activities or whatever the means of self-expression was as much about catharsis or distraction from negative thought patterns or painful real-life situations as it was about building skills and steps to self-esteem and confidence. I have studied psychology, sociology and other social sciences to develop integrated programmes and as part of that I have trained in the therapeutic use of mindfulness.

My own interest, love and respect for Irish traditions means I approach this book as an opportunity to explore. It is as much my journey as it is a journey I invite you to partake of therapeutically or, indeed, spiritually. I am not a guru on a mountain, dispensing pearls or kicks in the eye. I am within the human condition and continually undertake journeys and exercises to explore my own spiritual and psychological awareness. I do have experiences and awareness that I share through my writings here, but you may find a different solace or foothold in some of the seanfhocail – that is great if you do. It is the trigger point that is most important. The exercises and actions will help – but it is your life, your own roadmap. I do not say follow me. I do not say *I* can solve it for you – although I hope this book helps. I intend it to be helpful. But you steer your own ship, you climb your own rocks, you feel your own footing – that is how to live. You must take your own journey and solve your own self. I am not the mountain – I am my own mountain. This book is not the mountain. If anything, life is the mountain. You are your own mountain.

This book is an opportunity for me to explore what Zen masters may call *kenshō* – 'seeing essence' or looking into one's nature. In my case, this means looking into my cultural heritage – the seanfhocail. In doing so I invite you to walk a little with me, for it is a pathway to mindfulness and to psychological wellbeing and spiritual awareness. But the pace you take is your own, the stops you rest at are yours to choose. It is a helpful road to the base camp; the mountain you will scale in your own time. Remember: by time is everything revealed.

What is mindfulness?

As children, we may have heard the word mindful, in the context of, for example, 'be mindful that I need you back early to help' or 'be mindful of that stray dog' – and so we come to associate it with 'remembering' and, to a degree, with 'alert caution'. And indeed, there is a portion of both within mindful practice and mindful living, especially if we take caution to be attentive. But it is not about filling your mind with situations or factors that need attending to – that approach is having a 'mind full' of thoughts and to-do lists. No, being mindful is simply to be present, to be aware. Not self-aware in a self-conscious way; there is no need to analyse and react. It is about experiencing the moment, being truly yourself in that moment, in the context of being fully alive and participating in what you are doing or where you are. You may respond to what is going on, you may feel the experience of it, but you don't have to react. You can be you, you can *be* – you do not have to 'act' or 'become' anything – your true self gets to experience the moment and you get to be, in that moment, your own true self. Mindfulness is alertness to the present moment ... but in that present moment you truly live. No daydreams, no hang-ups – pure life as it happens.

Mindfulness is more than a stress management technique, although it is globally popular as that (and if that's your reason for picking up this book, the techniques within will guide you there). You can utilise mindfulness to catch your breath, to slow the pace and find some inner peace, but it offers so much more – spiritually, psychologically – and it even impacts positively upon physical heath. Before we explore the more, let's look at the immediate.

The modern world is fast-paced and stressful. When we charge through life reacting to everything, we are all about the reactions and the experience, not the true reality. Mindfulness slows the charge and allows us to respond rather than react, to witness in the present rather than moving between past recollection and leaping forward to make sense of our lives and ourselves. Caught between forward planning and nostalgia – where are you right now? Are you actually living your life? Or are you mentally flicking back and forth without ever truly taking in the experience? Fast forward, rewind, fast forward, rewind, pause a bit, fast forward again – are you experiencing your life and yourself as a film? Are you playing over the same tired dramas and stresses, are you brainwashing yourself in the process? Is it all in your head – the mind full? There is an alternative – being mindful.

Being mindful is simply being aware of what it is you are doing while you are doing it. You are reading a book now. The words on this page are understood by the language centre of your brain. You are conscious and sentient. You are standing, sitting in your favourite chair, on the commute home, lying on your bed, sitting under a tree. Whatever your surroundings, wherever you are, you have just cognately scanned it or opened the file of it. How about doing that with your other senses? Are your feet on the ground? If so, feel them make contact with the solidness of the floor or earth. How is your back against the chair? Experience how the chair supports you. You are a physical being in a physical reality – you are engaged in the mental process of reading and responding to the words, but your reality is that you are alive, a part of the living world. Take a breath, feel the air as you inhale it through your mouth or nose and experience the exhale. Take a deliberately deeper one – don't worry if people are nearby, they are caught up in their own worlds. That breath, that process of breathing, is what keeps you alive and it is also the easiest way to switch on mindfulness. Coming to your senses is what helps you come to your senses. There is no delusion or fast forwarding when you take the moment to become aware of the breath in and the breath out. No matter how stressful the day, or where you physically are, those breaths are life, real life. Mindful life.

Being aware and alive in this moment, as you read on and breathe naturally, means you are well capable of being aware that you are sitting, walking, running, listening to a friend, smelling a rose, cooking a meal or even washing the dishes. It's all life, every moment of it is your life. Why ignore it for the clutter of random thoughts and your fantasy film? The brilliant thing is that when you engage with life on the mindful level you experience more of life. It is not that dishwashing becomes a Zen experience every time, but living through the chore (as well as the treats) gifts a sort of mind control. Returning to the smell of the rose or the warm dishwater focuses and sharpens the mind/body/spirit so that when emotions or stress arise you can return to yourself and not get swept away by it all. The overwhelming bits of life will not be so overwhelming; or, better yet, we can make the overwhelming experiences be the awe-inspiring ones, instead of the devastating or distracting ones. Those thoughts that arise are not suppressed, they are noticed and moved on from, and there is no judgement. Just acknowledgement and acceptance.

I want you to try a trick – really try hard to focus and act accordingly. There is only one thing I am asking: Do *not* think of a polar bear. Do *not* under any circumstances picture in your mind a polar bear. Go!

So what did you do? Just like everybody else, your mind pulled out the polar bear snapshots. Your brain cannot stop thoughts, but you can chose to not linger. If I had said 'look, there is a polar bear', you may or may not have glanced over, you may or may not have given it some thought, you may have looked – noticed and acknowledged – and then continued about your business. That is how mindfulness works – OK, there is a polar bear. Next. OK, I am feeling a bit sad. Next. OK, I am anxious. Next. No need to dwell on anything. Next. This does not mean you become flippant or deadened, it simply means that you can filter out the noise and nonsense – so that instead of distractedly thinking about the to-do list, you can recognise that the polar bear is picking up speed and you can remember how to start the snowmobile.

When you have thoughts, notice that you have thoughts, and then return to being aware of what you are actually doing. When you are emotional, just notice the emotion – don't try to deepen it and don't try to push it away – just come back to awareness of what you are doing. Your mind has a tendency to drift, but mindfulness is not the constant vigilance required to watch out for that stray dog. It's not that you have to be 'on' 24/7, but that you can switch on when you need to. If you drift you will catch it and come back to the task in hand. You will be more efficient, which is why many companies send their employees on mindful courses, but think-tanks and pseudo-sweatshops aside, this new efficiency is all about *you* getting the most from life. From *your* life.

Mindfulness and wellbeing

In recent years, mindfulness techniques have become validated and utilised as tools for mental and physical health by health professionals and support groups globally.

Mindfulness improves mental health by giving us control over our minds, allowing us to choose to calmly respond or simply let go of thoughts arising before they become deep-seated feelings. The acceptance and letting-go processes in mindfulness cut out the aversion and avoidance cycles that add to psychological disturbances, stop the thoughts from becoming feelings and forming an emotional hook in your brain, changing how you experience the world. The breathing techniques are grounding, and embracing forgiveness, kindness and gratitude can reframe self-worth and also perception of the world.

Counsellors and psychotherapists often recommend mindfulness meditation to treat depression, anxiety disorders, addiction and substance abuse, eating disorders, self-harm and other obsessive-compulsive behaviour.

Mindfulness practices improve physical health by relieving stress, lowering blood pressure, releasing endorphins, improving sleep, and providing a sense of wellbeing and happiness. GPs and support groups often advocate mindfulness for a range of medical conditions. Apart from the physical benefits of summoning a sense of wellbeing, mindfulness lets you know and be yourself rather than being defined by your illness – mental or physical. Mindfulness takes away a mind full of adversity and emotional clutter and allows a purer you to find peace, clarity and resilience – to have the capacity for life. And there is nothing more healing than that.

Mindfulness and spirituality

On a spiritual level, what is now known as mindfulness has its roots in Buddhism and Hinduism and other echoes in many religions and mystical traditions around the cultivation of an enlightened awareness. In the Buddhist tradition it is *sati* – part of the noble eightfold path and central to the teachings of the Buddha. It features in the Upanishads and other Hindu scripture. It is also the backbone of the Christian contemplative tradition. Awareness/*sati*/mindfulness is both the means and the end to the enlightenment that the spiritual selves of all faiths seek – it is the thread of loving compassion that unifies us all, it is, to use a Western term, the grace of God. You may have previously encountered it for yourself in moments of prayer, chanting, meditation, contemplation, yoga or stillness. It is the 'at-one-ness'. It is being awake and aware of your living self presently engaged with the divine, and also of your own divine self. Mindfulness is as relevant a way to pray as it is a way to cope with a busy life.

Mindfulness and full potential

To live to your full potential is to live – to really live. We often confuse living with doing and not being. Parties, adventures, action – by all means pack your life full of wonderful experiences, but remember to experience each one. Mindfulness brings life to sitting on your front doorstep, to washing your hands, to taking the dog for a walk – imagine what it would do for traversing the steppes, showering beneath a waterfall or watching the wolves watching you. Mindfulness hones your grasp on reality and so deepens each experience. You don't have to circumnavigate the world to feel you have lived a life – being in the world is an adventure in itself. Being there as the seasons change in your back yard is as amazing as seeing a leaf unfurl or change colour anywhere in the world, because with mindfulness it is you and the leaf experiencing reality in the moment – a location is not necessary to bring awe into the equation.

Your full potential means really being there; being present, alert and awake to the life happening around you. Be there for your child's birth, be there for your parents' death, be there for all of your life – that is living – joy, pain, experience – that is life. That is living up to your full potential.

So whatever your intent – spiritual mindfulness, stress-relief mindfulness, addiction-control mindfulness, productive mindfulness – it is being aware of what you are doing in the moment of doing that delivers it. So be spiritual, be calmer, be free of desires and actively engaged with living. Be your true and full potential self.

Mindful tools

As an obair do fachtar an fhoghluim; learning comes through work. If you bought this book, you are looking to work on yourself – to work on your 'self' – to find the skills of mindfulness and have a better quality of life. On the way to being your true full potential self, the following tools may be useful.

Conscious awareness

Conscious awareness is the aim of mindfulness – it *is* mindfulness. It is also the way to attain mindfulness. So it is both a practised skill and a living state. Conscious awareness is simply being present in the moment, being present to each moment, moment by moment – that intent/action is the means and end of mindfulness. Simply become aware of what is happening or what you are doing. Use your senses to connect physically to the moment – is your skin warm or cold, are there fragrances, sounds – this makes the experience both physical and mental. If your mind and body are aware of what is happening right now, your spirit will meet this moment too.

Make an everyday experience mindful. If it's a shower, feel the water on your skin, the temperature and pressure, smell the fragrance of your body wash or shampoo – it is full of experience, not just a simple cleansing task. If you are cooking a meal, you can be present too, not just alert to not burning it, but alert to the sounds and aromas of cooking, to the skills of peeling, chopping, stirring, etc. Enjoy the process, or at the very least do it awake – fully experience it and live it.

Live and experience every process. There is nothing too mundane to be mindful with or nothing so special that it cannot be experienced mindfully – without having to evaluate and overthink. Conscious awareness is not having to concentrate in that manner, like an intellectual exercise. It is being aware. Awake. Present. You can always follow your breath to focus your mind from distracting thoughts. More on that further on.

Being consciously aware of what is happening in that moment is both the intent and the achievement. We are not seeking special moments – our life is a flow of moments, and to live in the moments is to live. So be conscious brushing your teeth in the morning, be conscious of the pillow beneath your head before you drift off to sleep at night. Be conscious breathing, walking, sitting. Be conscious of your lived moments and the attending sensations – this brings you into life. If you can enrich yourself with conscious awareness of making the bed or washing a plate, wait until you consciously eat your favourite meal, or consciously swim in the sea, consciously sit under a tree, consciously make love. You are not seeking enhanced pleasures or desperately trying to find more happiness and less pain – you are just looking to live. If you truly live rather than fantasise and daydream and sleepwalk through life, then you will have really experienced life, so be conscious in your moments – that is mindful living. That is the way to live. The following tools are ways to train and attain that conscious awareness.

Following your breath

Now that you have made the decision to be mindful or switch on your conscious awareness, the next job in hand is breath control. It will take time, and you may have to work at it, but not only does learning come through work, but working makes it real. Throughout this book I will make reference to the tools in this section, and in particularly to following your breath. Conscious awareness of breathing means following your breathing, but it is not a chore, it is a skill. You will master it and you will improve your life with it. Here is how to do it.

Sit still or stand tall, wherever you are. Be comfortable. Keep breathing as normal – just become aware of your breath. You may notice it in your nose, throat, chest or mouth. Just notice and pay attention to the reality that you are breathing in and out. Now focus on the inhale, feel it going in. Notice the exhale, feel it going out.

Become consciously aware of your breathing pattern. You don't have to slow it or alter it – just follow the inhale. Being with the exhale brings your focus to the process of breathing, instead of white-water rafting through your thoughts and emotions. It is the instant switch, the instant control mechanism, the uncomplicated now. Experience your inhales and your exhales. Become aware of the rising of your chest or the flaring of your nostrils but keep following the in and out of your breath.

Follow your breath, not your thoughts. If a thought crops up, let it happen, and come back. You may manage to follow a few breaths before your mind starts to drift, and you realise you are thinking about household insurance or what's for dinner or that twist in last night's soap opera. You can just come back to the breaths and take a time out from those other, meandering thoughts. Feel the inhale, the drawing in of air to your lungs, experience the exhale as you release the breath. In, out, in, out. That old thought is long gone, and you are consciously breathing. This is how to control thoughts.

As time moves on and you practise more conscious breathing, you will be able to train your brain to focus better when you call on it to do so. The more you do this the better it gets. You can do it for a few seconds any time you want to find the moment or escape the negative and disarm repetitive thoughts. You can also do dedicated timed sessions – five minutes before breakfast, five minutes at lunch. You may even do twenty minutes in a meditation setting. You will evolve and hone your practices into what suits you.

Breath awareness is also part of meditation, but it can be done standing, walking, waiting for a bus, sitting on a train, cycling or hanging out washing. It is not a dangerous process and it does not hypnotise you – you won't steer the bicycle off the track, miss the bus or drop the baby. It is just breathing, but mindfully – aware, not drowsy. In meditation we can use breath control to bring about calm, to lower blood pressure and stress, to slow the pace – relaxation is relaxation, and sleep is sleep, but breath control is both tranquillity and dynamic life experience. Because some people only know *on* as active and *off* as unconscious, they find for a time that slowing down makes them sleepy – if you worry that conscious breathing will make you drop the baby, then practise when your arms are free. You can skip it when you're preparing *fugu* for family and friends. You use it when you want it.

Practising breath control in meditation is great training for non-meditation circumstances. Breath control is really mind control. We are not always looking to dismiss thoughts, but to watch them arise and pass by without having to latch on and follow them all day. So breathing helps the mind stay focused and not follow the emotions and thoughts that arise in our everyday lives.

Mastering meditation

Meditation lowers levels of the stress hormone cortisol and engenders serenity and surety of purpose in non-meditation scenarios. But in the beginning, it can be a daunting task to take up or a tricky skill to master. Here are some tips to overcome those problems.

Step one – begin. Forgive the cliché, but all journeys really do begin with a single step and you have to start somewhere, so a single step is real action. Don't try to do a twenty-minute sitting meditation first time. Get the fundamentals first. Follow your breath, and when you notice you are thinking and not following your breath, return to your breathing. Allow yourself three distractions – three times to wander off while focusing on your breath. That's enough for now. Come back to it later. You are training your brain to return to focus and wander less. You want to feel that you have mastered it three times instead of failing one hundred times, so doing short bursts of *focus, wander, return* is building capacity. You can lengthen the duration as you go. Work up to a confident sixty seconds. Then a stress-free two minutes. Soon you can handle five minutes, then thereafter it's however long feels right.

Step two – forgive yourself. Meditation is not about never being distracted during a sitting, it is about catching the wandering and returning to the focus. Returning to the experiential rather than indulging the evaluating nature of your mind. Don't feel bad that you are wandering. Each wander is an opportunity to return, and it is the returning that trains the brain. Sometimes you are a whole shopping list down before you realise you have wandered, then you spend time reprimanding yourself – stop wasting time on guilt or pressure. Just come back to the breathing, chanting or focusing technique. The more you return, the more you will hone the skill and soon you will be catching yourself long before you have got two items on the grocery list.

Step three – don't let it be a chore. This is a skill for life, but it is also something that can be engaged in without heavy context or even as a way to unwind – even though it delivers much more than that. It's good to see it as something nice to do for yourself rather than another task on the checklist of an already busy day. It's helpful to have a routine, but it's also OK to be flexible and come to it when you get the chance. Think of it like a time out, like listening to some music, having a cup of coffee or taking a five-minute stroll to gather yourself. Make it more of a reward than a chore – that way you will not only continue with it but find the zone quickly when you sit into it. Take the pressure out of the equation and enjoy. Take the work out of it and let it put the life back into you.

Physical effects of meditation

With meditation, the idea is not to stop your mind from wandering – you don't have to become thoughtless. The idea is to become aware that you are wandering and return to the breathing, or to the meditation mantra – back to the now of whatever you are doing. It turns out this practice has some positive effects on neural pathways.

There have been several scientific studies on how meditation and mindfulness affect the neurological pathways in the brain. What the findings suggest is that the process of focusing on a single thing – your breath, a mantra or a mindful practice – and returning to it whenever the mind wanders off builds connections in neural pathways. The more you do it the more the circuit is reinforced. You can literally rewire your brain and your ability to focus, enhancing your capacity for concentration.

There have also been studies that show how meditation and mindfulness affect the physical and psychological self. What these studies suggest is that moods and emotions are better regulated, the immune system is strengthened, willpower is intensified, stress is reduced and the body's innate healing capabilities are energised.

For more about the effects of meditation on the brain and the physical self, see the Further Reading section at the back of this book.

Sitting meditation

There are many types of meditation: some where you chant a mantra to focus the mind on a single sound or phrase, some where you take in the stillness or sink into relaxation like a pebble falling to the bottom of a pool, and some where you use visualisation to engage your senses (you breath in the forest air, dip your fingers in the imaginary stream or feel the sand beneath your feet). All are valuable, but the simplest one of all is to just sit and follow your breath. It is the one I practise most and recommend to all. Just sit and follow your breath, observe thoughts arising, acknowledge them, but don't give them consideration or analysis, just see them and watch them go. No judgement, no action is required, just return to your breaths and soon you are relaxed and in the moment.

Sitting meditation is a good time out. It is a great way to recharge the batteries but it is also a way to hone breath and mind control. No equipment is required, there's no location to get to. It is possible at any time and for durations that suit you.

Walking meditation

A walking meditation can be nothing more than walking consciously – being aware of the movement of your body, connecting with the now of your steps. This is not a deliberately slow walk (although that too is a good way to intentionally take in the views and sounds of your journey), it is just a walk, at any pace but mindfully exercised. The connection with the action of walking as a way to become present is not arduous and it is easy to make it part of your routine or cues.

As you walk, simply become aware of your body in movement, noticing how your feet move you on, noticing and paying attention to your feet touching and leaving the ground. Thoughts may arise, but come back to your movement, to your feet touching and leaving the ground. Walking or strolling is a way to catch up on thoughts for many people, so conscious walking can be harder to master than you think for more than a short distance. But with practice comes mastery and soon you can consciously walk around the block or through a park or along the seashore – alive in every moment of it. Some people utilise following their breath while walking or bringing their consciousness to the single thought/realisation of 'I am walking' – that technique is good too.

The intent is to walk mindfully, following your progression, not your thoughts – awareness of walking is a walking meditation. Maybe you like to go for strolls or are more active, taking long walks or hillwalking – you can elect to make part of the experience a walking meditation, as little as five minutes or as much as 50%. Your call. But soon, just as those neural connections are made and strengthened, you will begin to get an enhanced experience of the entire walk.

Walking around holy wells and up sacred mountains was and is an important part of pre-Christian and Christian traditions in Ireland. Walking is a form of intentional prayer, a sacrifice of movement, a dedication of energy. Pilgrimages the world over in all faiths demand movement, the physicality of journeying mirroring a spiritual or inner journey. We move to change. So walks with chants, prayers, mantras or the intent to exchange energy with the world or the divine are great to partake in too. Walking, sitting, reading, drinking tea, being alive to it – that is prayer.

Sensation awareness

Getting in touch with your senses is a brilliant way to come into the immediacy of life – to 'be' right now. Touch, taste, smell, seeing, hearing – these are our radar system. They are how we sense danger, find food, connect with loved ones, how we experience and navigate life. Hardwired direct to the brain, they are the experience generators. While you are reading this, you are looking, your brain is taking in the words and your lifetime of experience is making sense of the sentences or validating/dismissing the content – so your senses are being utilised by your thinking/ conceptualising brain. If you are not sitting, then go find a chair before continuing to the next paragraph.

Now, how about we push a button in the brain, and begin to experience reality? Become aware of the weight of your body in the solidity of the chair. Clench and release, become aware of your thighs and calves, feel the presence of your legs, wiggle your toes. Are your feet on the ground? Is your back supported? Your brain is reading your body and alerting you to the fact that you are not just a sentient being engaged in a cognitive process, but a physical being in a physical world. Let the chair take your full weight – feel yourself held and supported by it. Your solid body. The solid chair. You are sitting on an object feeling and experiencing yourself sitting on an object – that is the reality of now. Stay with it a while, following your breath if you like – connect with the reality you are in. Stop reading and go with it. You are really here in this moment, sitting on a chair. Feel it for a while, experience this real sensation in real time.

Now that you have come back to reading you can read on in the awareness that you are real. We often read to escape – to leave the body in favour of the mind. Being aware that there is a cool breeze or warm room while you read will not diminish the reading experience. It is *you* reading, not your brain just following a stream of words.

After a long day I like to open the cap on some essential oil and inhale – that limbic flood of scent energises me. If it's not too late in the day, I can get that from a fragrant plant in the garden. I can get it from a bar of chocolate, an apple, anything fragrant – it is not even the scent itself, but the sense of smelling. You can use any of your senses to bring you to a sensation rather than a thinking/analytical moment – rub the back of your neck, listen to birdsong or the roar of traffic – it doesn't matter. It is the activation of sensation awareness that triggers your experience of that split second of smelling, seeing, touching, tasting or hearing. Following your breath is sensation awareness. Mindfully walking is sensation awareness. Conscious eating is sensation awareness. Sensation awareness is mindfulness.

You are receiving all this information from the real world anyway, but your mind is running that programme on low priority as your thoughts demand more attention. Being mindful turns up the power on receiving the real and in doing so turns up your power to experience it – to really be present in that moment. In this moment. Now.

Conscious observation

Conscious observation is also sensation awareness. It is looking, but really looking. Not looking at, not looking through, not just seeing something, but observing it and taking it fully in. The poets may talk of drinking in a sunset, and sunsets are great, but try it with a mundane object – say a coffee cup or a hammer. You can think of its function, feel its weight, notice its unique shape, its design, how it relates to you – but then look at it. Fully see it. Know it.

Seeing it this way, as if for the first time or with renewed appreciation, is a powerful exercise in experiencing objects. If the coffee cup or hammer comes to life, and you are alive with it, then there is the presence of awe. When you were a child, there was awe and fascination, exploring, discovering, experiencing. This is that again. Go look at the world.

I take the opportunity to enjoy and find awe in looking at mountains, clouds, the moon and flowers. I give them attention and they reward me. I enjoy going to galleries and am awed by the visual experience and technical detail in a painting or sculpture, by the subject matter and by each brush stroke. Looking this way really gets the brain going, and pattern recognition releases endorphins, so beyond the mindful opportunity it also delivers a physical sense of wellbeing and aliveness. Take the chance when you can to notice and 'be' – be in that observation, be in that moment. Coffee cup or Caravaggio, they all gift consciousness.

Conscious listening

Conscious listening is not just hearing sounds, but listening to them. Mindfully listening to music, the dawn chorus or even the hum of your refrigerator is activating. Sometimes music can be associated with emotions, or songs have a resonance with your life that can bring you to recollection and thought. As an exercise, try a new piece of music – something you can listen to for the first time, that you can explore and find that endorphin release. We may hear the dawn chorus on the way to bed or on the way to work, but do we listen to it, tune in and fully experience it? It is not pre-recorded, it is live, happening only in that moment. Yesterday's was different, tomorrow's will be different again. Listen to it, for this moment, hear its originality, find its rhythms and patterns, let the awe *be* and be with it. The hum of the refrigerator or the sounds of traffic may not seem to be awe-inspiring, but they are an opportunity to become conscious, present and alert to what is occurring right now. The focus is clarity. The clarity is in the pureness of the moment.

Now, just stop and listen, wherever you are – on a busy train, in a library, a bookshop, at home – just stop and listen for two minutes. You don't have to select a sound, just listen.

Now, try it again, but this time don't judge or analyse the sounds, simply hear them, fully hear them. If thoughts arise, let them pass and become conscious that you are listening and hearing – this is experiencing the real world. The noisy clatter, the silence, the subtle sounds that show that silence is not empty, but alive too. It may be a soft hum in the distance or it may be your beating heart. Experience that – experience being alive. That moment is mindful awareness.

Compassion and kindness

It is not enough to know that we should only cross the road when the signal lights change. We need to know that we should cross when they change from red to green. Half the picture is just not good enough. But often in life we think we have the whole picture, when really we have only been given or inadvertently received an incomplete message. Worse still, we may even be passing it around as gospel. When it comes to compassion it is important to understand the right frequency.

My secondary school education was through the Christian Brothers and they had outreach programmes with disadvantaged communities. We were often asked to bring in non-perishable food and old clothes or blankets for care parcels, and there were always charity boxes, raffle tickets and sponsored walk forms to bring home. The catchment area for the school was a disadvantaged area, so the running joke back and forth amongst my classmates was 'Did you get those beans, because I think I got your peas?' Hunger wasn't being alleviated – we were just swapping groceries among ourselves, but for some of us it helped to find a sense of community and in others it fanned anger at the inadequacy of it all. One might ask if the project was compassion or delusion. I still have mixed feelings about it, but even though there was pressure on families to give, beyond that emotional blackmail and sense of panic, the eventual sacrifice was an act of loving kindness towards another family, next door or up the street.

In fifth and sixth year, we were asked to exercise our compassion and volunteer with some of the hands-on outreach – deliver the care parcels, wash windows for the elderly, etc. One year I volunteered to do 'soup runs' – delivering soup and sandwiches to the homeless across Dublin in the run-up to Christmas. It took place on Friday and Saturday nights between 10 p.m. and 1 a.m. I had a few weekends under my belt when I met a senior figure of the charity, and she said to me that I was doing wonderful work for these 'poor lost souls'. That kicked me in the guts – *poor lost souls*. 'Poor' was not an acknowledgement of poverty, it was an evocation of pity, and 'lost souls' – who says the homeless are denied the Kingdom of God? What was John the Baptist's job? Where was Christ's fixed abode? I replied, 'There but for the grace of God go you'. I wasn't asked back the following week. I had let my anger rise. Perhaps I should have shown her some loving kindness, but I thought it more appropriate at the time to allude to the fuller picture. To my seventeen-year-old self, the homeless were not lesser beings, not less devout or spiritually empty. They were not cast out of God's love, nor were they wayward or being punished. On the way home, I thought about how it is that sometimes those in charge of soothing society's ills have never really experienced any ill. If you have ever been hungry, ever been emotionally wounded or in need of some solace, then you will know the difference between pity and compassion. That's what I mean by the right frequency.

Practise compassion, not pity. Compassion – not even empathy. True compassion. True compassion is a loving kindness that should be extended towards all those in need – the homeless person and the pity-mongers alike. Really, to everyone on the planet. That's hard, I know, because there are so many fools and unpleasant people out there. But even they are deserving of God's love, of a moment of regard from you.

How you do it is simple – just think of someone you love or hold dear like a niece, a sibling, your child or your mother. Become aware of the kindness towards them that wells up in your heart. You are energised by that. Right now, you have that pouring through you, radiating from you. It is abundant and never-ending, and you have an endless supply. Let it radiate beyond you, share it psychically with the person you are thinking of. You can mentally blow them a kiss, or imagine you are brightening their aura or putting a smile on their face – that's the energy exchange of loving kindness. You have boundless amounts of this energy. Why not picture a few friends and send them a smile, or picture a colleague or neighbour in need and send them some positive energy – some loving kindness, some true compassion. This is *loving thy neighbour*. You can throw some coins in the next beggar's cap, but also extend friendliness – acknowledge them in all their humanity with all your humanity – in the everything that is God, this person is one of the many. Extend that feeling of warmth to strangers on the street, to people on the other side of the world you will never meet. Someone is extending it to you right now.

Don't forget to give yourself some warmth from time to time too. Stop beating yourself up about not being on top of your game or failing to be mindful in every single moment. We all make promises we can't keep, bite off more than we can chew. We are human. Love your humanity. Accept yourself – faults and good intentions included. You can be compassionate to yourself and to the world. It is good to give, and it is also good to forgive. Forgive yourself.

Acceptance

Acceptance is not defeat. It is acknowledging where you are now. It is realising the reality of the situation or the way of the world. You don't have to resign yourself to it, but seeing it clearly is a way to surmount it, if need be. Ups and downs, swings and roundabouts – these are all part of the nature of things and are what makes the fabric of life a rich tapestry. The French may say *C'est la vie*, but the Irish say *Is iomaí cor sa tsaol* – there is many a twist in life. There is no need to dwell on those twists. We accept and move forward.

Gratitude

Saying 'thank you' can be as much social etiquette or indoctrinated good manners as any genuine heartfelt gratefulness. Are we really thankful? Sometimes in our life it is hard to find things to be thankful for. Well, that's the lie we tell ourselves to stay miserable. There is plenty to be thankful for. Even awareness of the pain we are in – gratitude can be the catalyst needed to get out of it. Be grateful that you have the clarity to know you need to change the situation.

We live in a society of unconsciously delivered or throwaway thanks – which are as vacuous and impactful as a robotic 'have a nice day' or 'missing you already', no matter how enthusiastically delivered. So we may undervalue the verbalisation of gratitude, but it's time to invest it with meaning again. If you are to be mindful, then consciously appreciate and acknowledge the good things in life, the kindnesses you are shown and the services provided. Next time you say 'thank you', mean it or leave it. If you find you are having to leave it, it's time to explore why you can't find it in yourself and remove that obstacle. It's an obstacle to growth and a fully experienced life.

So we can easily be thankful that we got the all-clear, that the wedding went off without a hitch and for all the other big moments, but it is gratitude for the little things, the mundane things, the everyday things that brings not only mindful action but also a positive impact on our sense of wellbeing.

So do you really 'love' that television show, or do you just like it a lot? You can be as grateful for the like as for the love, for the reality as the exaggeration. No harm in being grateful for something as disposable as TV – it may be something that helps you forget your troubles or exercise your intellect and so worthy of being thankful for. I am not advocating that we immerse ourselves in television and anaesthetise ourselves to the real world. But I am personally thankful that there are gardening, nature and science shows on television, and they are my treats. I have, in periods of my life, lived for years without television or radio and I did read, meditate, visit galleries, real places and also socialise more. But now that there is a TV currently in my home I am grateful for the opportunity – albeit remotely and editorially delivered – to experience a year in the life of the tundra wolf or to learn what is new in neonatal surgery. Even things that are experienced remotely can make you grateful that conservation and new lifesaving techniques exist in the real world. If you are just caught up in sport or soap operas, it's OK to be grateful for those distractions too. It's all about seeing the reward and acknowledging it. So the next time a driver lets you out, or a waiter clears the table, you can experience and share the gratitude. The next time you get good news or just remember how good it is to be alive, you can really send that gratitude out into the universe.

Many studies have found that experiencing gratitude can significantly increase your sense of wellbeing – that being grateful for both the good things and the mundane things can protect you from stress, negativity, self-pity, anxiety and depression. Part of this is a positive-to-negative ratio: if you go around feeling sorry for yourself or irked at somebody else's inconsideration, then you are keeping that frame of mind and only a lottery win would shake you out of it. But by acknowledging the things that are going right – the multitude of them in every day – by being glad and grateful about them, you can tip the scales over into a joyous frame of mind. For more about the proven effects of gratitude, see the Further Reading section at the back of this book.

Positive action

Everything about mindfulness is a positive action. In deciding to live a better life, to find and explore your full potential, positivity is the path and the destination. The more positivity we generate, the more we find it around us, and the more tangible it becomes. Positive action is doing the right thing, yes, but it is more than that. Positive action is doing something mindfully, but it also generates more of itself.

Positive action is also intent. You might not be feeling positive today, but if you smile you can flip that switch. Making a smile instead of a frown actually connects the positivity circuit. Make a smile now and hold it, become aware of the shape of your smiling mouth, of your cheeks, how it seems to open your eyes and feel that sensation across your face. If you hold it long enough, and it may only take a few seconds, you will find you want to smile for real. It's OK to smile for real. The other great thing about smiles is that they are as contagious as yawns, so your smile can make others smile. We can practise loving kindness with a simple smile. We can energise ourselves with a simple smile.

The positive actions and exercises in this book are designed to bring you into the now. Some of them will take you out of your comfort zone, but many will put a smile on your face, if not outright joy in your heart. The positive actions you choose each day will allow your mind-body-spirit to sense that you are in a mode of happiness. That generates wellbeing and more sensations and awareness of happiness. More positivity leads to more positivity.

The more you increase your positivity the more automatic it becomes. Your destiny is to be a positive being, but you don't have to wait too long for destiny to meet your positive self. Don't get caught up in the moral compass of doing-the-right-thing, which implies a wrong thing, and thus guilt for not being continually right. Positive action is not the Ten Commandments; it is not even a rule to follow. It is experience and the birth of positivity through real action – it is not summoned like willpower, or brought forth like faith. It is *being*, unhindered by morality, guilt or shame, by motivation, goal-seeking or even sensation-seeking – positive action is the true dynamic of your soul. You will not have to second-guess yourself, you will not have to analyse or pass judgement – the freedom of self-expression will blossom. Then, everything you do will be positive action. If that's not something to smile about ...

Positive thinking

Positive thinking is a way to set the default to optimism rather than to pessimism. Some people are squeamish about showing optimism. It has, perhaps, connotations of naïveté, but the word optimism derives from the Latin word *optimus*, meaning 'best', and that is all we are doing when we exercise optimism – getting the best from the situation. Seeing the glass as half full instead of half empty tees you up for feeling gratitude for what you have, and not fear of what you lack.

Positive thinking can come in the form of personal affirmations, neuro-linguistic programming, or other motivational techniques, but it can also be simple optimism. That is just choosing (or developing the tendency) to see, acknowledge, believe, expect, intend or hope that things will turn out well, that all will come right. It is confidence in life. Positive thinking is not a high-wire act without a safety net. Positive thinking is knowing that the safety net is there, but also that you have done this a thousand times before, and it is just cautiously walking in a straight line. Mindfulness is often something as simple as walking in a straight line – consciously.

Positive thinking is not fantasising or mentally roleplaying idealised futures. Even though I advocate visualisation and mental dry-runs of scenarios to attain a positive approach, positive thinking also requires positive action – simply daydreaming the future is not being in the now. Prolonged positive fantasising can manifest as a misapplication of energy and non-actualisation of goals – the more you live in the happy bubble the less effort you will invest in realising the goal in reality. Positive thinking is muscle memory and the assurance and confidence to succeed and deflect setbacks – it is not absenting oneself from proactive behaviour. Visualise making it across, but once you step on that high wire, let your senses guide you.

Don't worry if you think you are a natural-born pessimist – that's just your programming thus far, and you can reset yourself. How you make positivity your default setting is to begin by reconsidering or reframing how you define experiences and events. Start dropping the tendency to dwell on the bad experiences or unpleasant events, and instead see those situations as learning experiences. You will learn something – OK, blind dates are not ideal for my sister's wedding, garlic pesto on toast is not the breakfast of champions on the day of a job interview – and if all you learn is not to make the same mistakes, then that's to the benefit of your future self. But you can learn more: Wow, my blind date really hit the bottle before hitting the groom – minus five points; but I was excellent in calming the hotel manager and my hysterical sister – plus ten points. Now you are five points ahead and not five points down. Fingers crossed, it will never be that dramatic, but you see what I mean.

If I have a project that is taking ages to get green-lit, I choose to see it as the time not being right and at least I have all the work done for when the perfect moment arises. I see setbacks as opportunities to perfect, reflect, refine and move closer to success. Personally, I don't dwell on 'it will never happen', because then it never will, and if it's not meant to happen, then you need to be ready for what will happen (or what you can make happen) and not stuck in the past. Drop it to get to the next one. If I can quote a fellow Irishman, Samuel Beckett: 'Ever tried. Ever failed. No matter. Try Again. Fail again. Fail better.'

Failing better eventually leads to success. Seeing the learning opportunity in the misfortune is what brings good fortune. Adopting this mind-set resets the pessimist to an optimist – to a getter of better.

Peak experience

Peak experience is not so much an activity as it is a pure moment of activated self. The term and intellectual definition of the experience has been ascribed to the American psychologist Abraham Maslow, who wrote extensively about what he called 'moments of highest happiness and fulfilment' that triggered or acted as 'an advanced form of perceiving reality'. Earlier scholars may have called it an epiphany, some even 'divine visitation', 'enlightenment' or even 'self-realisation'. It is the bubbling up of a blissful, carefree feeling of the totality of yourself and unity with the universe – it is switched-on-ness.

Peak experience can arise during meditation, mindful practice, sex, chanting or prayer, but also during athletic, artistic and natural experiences and other 'eureka' moments. It can be the moment when you work out the chord change in a song you are learning. It can be the moment you solve the missing link in your intellectual theory or science project. It can be the moment you see a tree as a living thing. It can be the smile on the face of your lover. Those transcendent moments of pure joy, those hits of elation, all those experiences that give you the overwhelming feeling of wellbeing – of being joyously alive.

I personally have found it most often through tantric sex, kundalini yoga, meditation and in creative self-expression, but I have also had it waiting for a bus, making a cup of tea and swimming a few lengths of the pool. Do those things that gift it, but also in the everyday and in every way, make a habit of peak experience. There comes a time when just thinking of peak experience delivers a peak experience.

To explore further the concept of peak experience, see the Further Reading section at the back of this book.

Mindful cues

The above is all well and good, but the secret to success is remembering to employ these actions. From time to time, life can get busy, even chaotic, and before you know it routines are deprioritised, and sometimes even when the crisis subsides you can find yourself having to work your way back up in increments to the discipline you had before. Creating cues – mindful triggers – is the answer. I have a shaving mirror with *smile* etched into it. I have a fridge magnet with 'best use of your time' printed on it and I have a note above my computer with 'Human BEING' written on it. Those written reminders trigger in me the intention to be joyous and mindful in the course of each new day. Such positive affirmations may work for you. Visual cues work too. I have a smiley-faced badge on my yoga bag that reminds me it is not a chore but a pleasure.

It can also be an everyday action that you set up to do deliberately and mindfully. Some days, I have no time for meditation or yoga, I may be in a different city or on a tight schedule, I may have to shower and run, or I may skip breakfast. But at some point during the day I will have a cup of green tea that I can sip and savour and mindfully experience – so at least once a day, no matter how hectic life is, the green tea is a trigger. Then, when the deadlines and intense days are over, I can return to a mindful shower, a mindful breakfast or a mindful walk in the garden.

In this book I talk about washing the dishes, going for a walk – everyday actions, the mundane moments of the day. Pick one such regular activity and make it your cue. Do it mindfully. Notice every aspect of it. This brings you into the now. This elevates the mundane to a living experience. Even a cup of tea can release grace and harmony. So can putting the groceries away.

So, like me, you can use reminders to be mindful and you can also have a daily chore you use as an opportunity. The visual and verbal cues are best decided by yourself as it is you they will awaken – fridges, bedside tables and bathrooms are good locations as you find yourself there daily. When it comes to a chore, you will find one that really works for you. To start with, how about for a week you brush your teeth mindfully – experience the movements of the brush, the taste of the refreshing toothpaste, the sensation of a clean mouth and the rejuvenation of your teeth, mouth and breath that is also the refreshment of your mind, body and spirit. That is being alive.

As you read on, through the seanfhocail and the exercises, you will be brought to this heightened aliveness – this mindful awareness – but then the book is over and you are potentially back into unchartered waters. The cues you create over the coming weeks and months will help you navigate for the rest of your life. Enjoy it. You may only live your life once – but once or ever renewed – the living is best lived fully.

Visualisation

Visualisation, sometimes dubbed 'creative visualisation', is a mental technique that uses the power of the mind – of our imagination – to manifest changes in our approaches to problems and cultivate success in certain scenarios. It can be thought of as mentally roleplaying the situation over and over, seeing a positive outcome and prepping yourself to succeed. It is utilised a lot by sports people who visualise the approach and tempo of penalty shootouts, perfect putts, faster serve returns, etc. It builds psychological muscle memory of perfected action and thus achievable success.

Think of the hours that pilots and astronauts spend in flight simulators. Visualisation is like that. It is working out the kinks with minimal risk. It is a way to notch up some practice. It is training the brain to function at its full potential. It is not wishing. It is not daydreaming. It is incorporating real action and actual determination to achieve your goals. It can accompany real physical practice too.

Opting to continually retreat to your happy place can stop you from achieving enough to secure a non-virtual happy place. Visualisation is not fantasising, it is honing thoughts and expectations into the confidence and capacity necessary to deliver in the real world, on the physical plane, in the moment required.

Some meditations call on you to visualise a beach or stream or to go through a scenario. These sorts of visualisation connect with the brain to achieve a good outcome. They are not daydreaming either; they are using the visual language of the mind to make psychological connections and improve our responses and thought-to-feeling experiences.

How to use this book

There are fifty-two proverbs in this book, one for each week of a year, be that a calendar year from January or a cycle begun at any time. Take the time to truly explore and benefit from the revelations. Starting this book in January or July makes no difference to the outcome. By time is everything revealed – it is the time that you apply that will yield the rewards. The idea is to bring you to sustainable mindfulness by exploring proverbs and experiencing the mindful and rewarding insights they bear. When you start or how quickly you finish is completely within your purview. The ideal time to start is whenever you are ready to start. However, as this book is about finding how to be in the now – why not now?

My experience from running mindfulness sessions – and the many years that I worked in education and training – is that increments work. You get time to incorporate new techniques into your way of life or adjust your way of life to a better place and pace to fully utilise new skills. To put this book into practise over a year gives you breathing space between each lesson, allows a fuller absorption and assimilation of the techniques and helps you process the changes. A year is a good pace – a firm commitment. This is, after all, for the rest of your life. *Nil ó mheud an phráinn nach lughaide na gnothuidhe* – the greater the hurry, the less the work – take your time and apply that proverbial lesson from the get go.

That said, commitment is more important than pace, so you need not be constrained to weeks if you perceive a whole year as too long to acquire the skills you urgently require. Not everyone will want to treat it as a course – though it is a journey – and not everyone can be patient enough to wait a week for the next insight. No judgement on that. You are who you are at this point and it is no sin to read this book cover to cover in a single sitting or over several days or even to leave it on the bedside locker and dip in periodically. While it is laid out at a weekly pace, its wisdom can be understood and applied at any rate you chose. If you chose a faster pace you will not fail. You may wish to read through this book once and then perhaps return at a later stage to reread at the regular intervals that are suggested. Just don't feel you have to speed read them – it is good practise to take it slow.

One a day or one a week. It is not so much about pacing yourself, although that is a valuable lesson in mindful living. It is more about 'deliberate nowness'. If you spend a day or a week pondering a proverb, returning to it as you would your mindful breath, or letting it percolate and unfold, then it will reveal its full potential. If you fly through six at a time, then you are just reading words and not getting to experience their vibrations. Slowing things down to focus on the deliberate nowness gets you into the moment of that phrase. Yes, if you are your wits end, if you are depressed or in spiritual crisis, there is urgency and action is required. Just don't mistake the kneejerk action/reaction for the more beneficial responding/resolving approach. To invoke an English language expression – more haste, less speed.

Getting the most from this book will help you get the most from life. You may intellectualise it – which can be more mind full than mindful – but its single objective is a guiding force and a way to train direction, intention and process, so that when you come to contemplate each proverb, you get it and there is no working it out. You can sit in the pleasure of that understanding. It is not some sort of intellectual smugness, like getting the quiz questions right, it is more that you hear the question as an invitation to answer it with your self-aware, loving, non-judgemental self or other facet of the divine-participating you that will be cultivated through this book. Beyond the wisdom of the words there are opportunities to put that wisdom into action – with exercises and actions accompanying each seanfhocal.

Some of the exercises in this book invoke immediate action, and others are layer-building. Like life, sometimes the most important thing is to take your time – but other times the most important thing is to jump. Knowing the difference is a blessing.

A note on exercises and action

Gnáthamh na hoibre an t-eólas is a proverb I particularly like – knowledge comes through practice.

While repetitiveness hones skills, the experience of actually doing can deliver the goods, so I have peppered this book with exercises and actions. The exercises are ways of acquiring a skill (breathing, focus, listening, other mindful techniques) or a way to move something on (dropping what is holding you back or developing a certain mind-set or attitude. The actions are opportunities to directly explore or experience a mindful moment in the everyday world. Actions such as going for a slow walk or hugging a tree become about shaking up your routine and making you 'experience', but that experience is about getting dynamic with all aspects of your life. Mindfulness is about really living, so why not live in those moments too? There will also be sitting still moments, but they are just as dynamic as they bring you to yourself, your unhindered self – free from kneejerk reactions and thought programmes.

These exercises and actions are optional, not compulsory. You may find them helpful, but you can also choose to encounter and embrace the wisdom of the seanfhocail in your own unique way. If the exercises and actions are not for you, that's fine. You may have experience with breathing exercises and yoga and the other techniques in this book, but you may also want to think of them as an opportunity to jump in. Warm water or cold water, if you want to swim across, you have to jump in at some point.

The exercise you do doesn't have to be the one recommended, but the more you go to the zone, the more you build muscle memory. I find it useful to do exercises every now and then as a way to physically participate or spiritually engage. Some people like to say prayers, some pray by lighting a candle. The exercises are ways of enjoying the richness of each experience. Drinking in a sunset, climbing a hill at dawn or just following your breath upon waking are all opportunities to live – if you are just starting out they are opportunities to help you live mindfully. Eventually you won't have to strive for it. Once upon a time, you had to learn how to see, to hear and respond, to crawl and then to walk – they are automatic now. So too will mindfulness begin to kick in on its own. The exercises and actions build the muscle memory. They get you fit and capable. You won't have to work so hard at it every day for the rest of your life – it's about wiring the circuits. I may not always have the luxury of being fully mindful during a lecture, meeting or book signing – when reactions rather than responses can arise or you have to call your analytical brain into play – but I can follow my breath in the moment before it commences and switch on the intent to be absolutely present. That is often the switch that stays on through the whole event – it lets me live the experience and be real in it too.

These exercises and actions are not only good opportunities to commit but also ways to activate your mindfulness directly, intently and immediately. Finding the now can be instantaneous or a process, but its nature necessitates that you attempt it *now*. So why not partake in an exercise or action as you find it and try the ones you like the best on a regular basis long after you have finished the book? The work may be all the better for the lack of haste – for the deliberate attention, for the mindful approach – but to use an another seanfhocal, *is in ithe na putóige atá an chruthú* – the proof of the pudding is in the eating.

The power of practice

The more you practice mindfulness, the more it becomes how you are and what you do naturally. You build metaphysical muscle memory, but you are not on autopilot – you are making precise movements with precise focus. Take martial arts, for example. It is not a dance, even though the thousands of hours of practice make it as exquisite as a dance, but learning the steps is only the framework for the true art – anticipation, concentration, reaction and response. Become a warrior through practice – not with aggression, but with a mind firing on all cylinders. You don't have to hunt or make your dinner with a sword, but carry the honour and the vigilance of the warrior into your practice – that is also mindful living.

The 10,000-hour rule proposes that approximately 10,000 hours of practice delivers mastery. Some advocate that anybody, even if they have no innate talent in a particular discipline, can complete 10,000 hours of deliberate practice and become an expert. Others advocate that some talent helps. But all agree that continual dedicated practice over time hones skills and enables mastery.

You won't have to sit following your breath for 10,000 hours. It is the cumulative factor of repeat meditations that facilitates breath control and the mindful experience of the breathing. But it is better to spend ten minutes meditating than it is to spend ten minutes feeling depressed, anxious and agitated. All those minutes add up, and you become the sum of them. So spend more time on the positive, become an expert in it and just be a very poor amateur at negativity.

To further explore the power of practice, see Further Reading at the back of this book.

The proverbs

Is trian de'n obair tus a chur

Making a beginning is
one-third of the work

So you have commenced – now the journey has begun.

The hardest part is to start, to conquer your fears or preconceptions, to step into the unknown.

Clap your hands – not to congratulate yourself – but for the sound of the clap; a single loud clap. This is an old Zen trick to announce the now, an old martial arts trick to concentrate the chi into the commencement of battle or into the focused discipline of the technique.

Now do it – clap your hands. Listen to the crack of it, feel the impact of it on your palms. The sound, the sting, the energy, the intent. Attending to the clap is a way to enter into mindfulness, into the now. Clap and be present. Clap now!

Action

The hand-clap challenge

For the next five days when you wake up – clap! Later, when you have lunch – clap before you eat. At night, before you get into bed – clap. Let each clap be a single loud and resonant clap. The first clap of the day announces that you are awake and participating. The second indicates that you are present and partaking of sustenance. With the last clap you invoke the restorative power of sleep.

After five days, the single clap will have become embedded in your consciousness as the start of 'alert participation'. Hereafter you can use it any time you need an instant reminder of your present self.

An gad is giorra don scornaigh is ceart a scaoileadh

One should first of all loosen the knot that is nearer the throat

Prioritise! First things first! What is your biggest obstacle to a mindful life? Too busy? Too angry? Too lazy? Too stupid?

The 'stupid' one always raises the hackles – use that energy. Negative energy such as anger can be a motivational tool or adrenalin surge to accomplish something – not only as a catalyst or engine of change, but as a transmutation of negative into positive. We need to own and master the bad as much as the good.

Use your determination for change to actually change. Stop planning for it. Do it. Sever that knot that binds you to a half-life – to a life of half potentials and unacted-upon promises to do it tomorrow. Don't put it off until tomorrow – do it now. Write down what that knot is. You know it. It's right at your throat this very second. Say it out loud. Acknowledge what is holding you back, and then write it down. Identifying it is the way to loosen its grip.

Some knots take work; some are simply untied in a second. Sometimes just seeing that you eat to replace love or don't make friends for fear of rejection is enough to recognise a cul-de-sac misconception that just needs to be reversed out of. Sometimes the dark thinking that you don't deserve happiness dissolves in the light of day, other times you may need to talk about it with a trusted friend or counsellor to fully pick that knot apart – it's prioritising it as top of the agenda that will bring success.

So if you need to, pin it on the fridge or the bathroom mirror and loosen it each day until you can fully breathe – fully live.

Exercise
Removing the impact of negative people

It may be an overbearing mother, a bullying sibling, a distant father, a horrible neighbour, a work colleague, a frenemy – whatever. Picture that person as a hologram before you, vibrant and alive, but not corporal – this is not their physical body; this is the symbolic manifestation of their psychic hooks in you.

Now walk through them. Do it in your mind's eye or physically take those steps forward. You will see that they could not hold you back – the hologram manifestation has no resistance, no grip, no power to stop you. You have all the control. Walk through them again, but this time, as you do, they will lose a bit of their integrity, lessen in colour, diminish in solidity. They are hollow. Feel your solid body. As it easily cuts through the shape in front of you, it breaks the hologram's hold over you.

Each time you step through the hologram, it weakens, becoming paler, feebler, until it is an almost translucent wisp. You have not physically harmed this person, but you have psychologically strengthened yourself. Look how weak this apparition is before you. You can walk through it one more time and blow it to dust. Don't be afraid of that. Show no mercy with negativity. Now kill it off. Disintegrate the negative energy and know you have done good.

An te chuireas, 'se baineas
He that sows will reap

—◆—

This seanfhocal is about cultivating positivity and attaining goals. It directly expresses the reward of positive action. Sow and you will reap. Do and you will be rewarded. It is a familiar concept, and we hear it quoted a lot. But do we really hear it?

To sow and reap is biblical. It features heavily in the Christian faiths and maybe it has lost some of its power consequently in that context. Certainly, from my early life in a Christian Brothers school, it was more along the lines of 'if you do bad you will get your comeuppance'. As you sow, so shall you reap – 'reap' suggesting that the grim reaper would come to get you for liking girls and bunking off mass. Instant karma. But that is not the meaning – instead, it is everything positive. It is just what you should be doing right now. While we must weed the negative, so too we must sow the positive – and sow for the future too. Instant karma can be good karma.

In reading this book and, where you can, following the actions or exercises, know that you are sowing seeds of personal growth and psychological stability, and you will ultimately harvest not just life skills but a life *full*. We often preoccupy ourselves with 'life fills' in lieu of a life full – those fills may be a soap opera you can't miss, the Sunday crossword, a glass of wine after a long day, the July sales, a bet on the Grand National, the ritual of a pedicure or the treat of a towel shave. These little diversions from the mundane are what we think of as life rewards, and yes, it is good to reward ourselves and to feel good, but for most people these fills are mistaken for a full life. A full life is not accumulated moments, it is the continuation of moments. It is being mindful, present, aware of the continuousness of our living experience. We don't have to lurch or drag ourselves from one reward to the next, we don't have to live for the weekend. Sow in your heart the promise to live every day – that does not mean more wine and more treats! To live every day is a much better reward than that. To live every day is to feel the full presence of life – mindfulness brings that alive.

Exercise
Sowing some positive intent

Gather some wildflower seed into the palm of your hand and take up a comfortable meditation position. Imagine all the goals you want to achieve. See yourself in each scenario – smiling and pushing your grandkids on a swing, in the changing room fitting into a smaller size, taking a picture on top of the mountain you just climbed. Let the seeds absorb those wishes. Energise those grains with your intent to bring those wishes to fruition – now go and sow them. Get up, go outside and sow them – on the wind or into soil.

Wildflower seed might just germinate and not only bring the symbolism a step further with living reminders, but will also ripple with positivity by bringing food for larval butterflies, nectar for bees and beauty to your locality.

You can also do the same exercise but with uncooked rice grains. With rice, it is a wholly metaphorical sowing. While it will not germinate, it has the value of real seed in that what you are actually sowing in the exercise is your positivity. You will harvest from this type of sowing too. Intent is all that matters. Think of how we throw rice at weddings for luck and to celebrate the new journey of marriage. Rice throwing is a celebration, and rice sowing is you celebrating your journey and providing future provisions for the path ahead.

Is maith an mustárd an sliabh
The mountain is good mustard

~<

This seanfhocal is about how work builds up an appetite. It is often said that food tastes better when you are hungry rather than when you are just eating because it is the designated time. We often shovel food in as fuel, like coal into old steam trains. We should stop and experience it. Mindfully enjoy each meal. But beyond that, there is further wisdom here: appreciation for endeavour and gratitude for its rewards.

Effort is rewarded. Know that.

The task of climbing the mountain gives you an appetite. It stimulates and enlivens. Understand that.

Engaging with nature can bring you into mindfulness. Experience that.

Exercise

Practise mindfulness outdoors

If you can, go somewhere scenic – the sea, the hills, a forest – someplace to stimulate you. If you can't get to the great outdoors, just get outdoors – a local park, your own garden, campus grounds, a walk around the block. Being outside is a great and pleasurable way of coming into the present. Feel the temperature of your skin, be aware of your breath, feel your footing. Encounter the sights, sounds and fragrances of nature – all good mustard for relishing the now.

Léig an donas chun deiridh,
a n-dúil s' nach d-tiocaidh se
choidche

Leave the bad luck to the last, in
hopes that it may never come

Pure optimism from the Irish psyche. We Irish often forget, owing to our history, that we are essentially a positive people. People of all nationalities make that same mistake.

Too often in life we prioritise the negative. The squeaky gate instead of the scenic walk is at the top of the to-do list. It's as if we are programmed to attend to the bad stuff first – but if we left it to last it might not even arise as we would fill the order of the day with positive stuff.

Part of it is how we are emotionally programmed – we dwell on the break-up and sense of loss rather than the newfound freedom and the potential of a new relationship. That is a shocking statement to some, but it is not diminishing the love you had – it is acknowledging it, acknowledging the relationship is over and acknowledging that you deserve love again. You lose your job – don't dwell on being unemployed for ever. Get motivated now to find the ideal job or to start your own business where you will get paid for your passion. The latest kitchen experiment was a complete failure – does that mean you can never cook again? Put the negative to the end of the list and get on with the good stuff in life.

Starting off with the positive and ranking it first may occupy the space long enough for you not to notice the negative.

Exercise
Count your hatched chickens

It's OK to count your hatched chickens to recount the good times and see the joy and fortune in your life. This notion of not counting your chickens before they are hatched is wise as it spares you disappointment, but you don't have to be overly cautious with the ones already hatched. They are the chirping success stories, and may even lay more golden eggs.

Think of the top five great achievements of your life. One of them may be climbing a tree when you were ten – it doesn't have to be climbing the corporate ladder. Whatever makes you proud. Write them down. Every now and then you can pull out this list before breakfast and count down the high points of your life. It reminds you of the successes, of the good luck. You can update the list as often as you like.

Anáil na beatha an t-athrú
Change is the breath of life

We often hear that a change is as good as a rest, but really, change is the breath of life.

This seanfhocal shouts it aloud – change is fundamental to life. While rituals like prayer, chanting, meditation and yoga are all spiritual tools grounded in beneficial reinforcement, embedding deep spiritual or psychological security by continual revisiting, we can also pray and attain this by doing something different – something new.

The exercises in this book that include stationary or repeating practices are engines of change – they will transform your life, but you can be freer too. Monday night yoga is brilliant, but remember to shake up your routine, or even spiritual practice can become a rut. Monday night yoga might for this week become Sunday morning yoga in the park.

Change truly is the breath of life. Humanity is altering all the time as we adapt to survive or as a consequence of how we choose to live. Evolution is continuing. Society moves on too, and – we pray – social justice moves with it. We are far from feudalism, but not far enough yet. We can become the change we want to see in the world, as Gandhi preached and practised. Change breathes life, and change is the process of life. We age, we alter, we grow in knowledge and skills, we experience different things – we keep moving and finding the new or we stagnate and stop.

Change occurs. It physically happens to our bodies and within nature, as the seasons remind us. Yes, all around us, change occurs. This is also true of the spiritual and psychological self. The evolution of our spirit is the immediate goal, and it is the intention of this book.

Action
Make a change

Actions energise your life, so take a risk. Shake it up – go dancing instead of bowling. Shake it up – get your hair cut differently. Make a change.

Ní fhaghann cos' na comhnaidh aon nídh

The foot at rest meets nothing

Doing nothing gets you nowhere. It is time to dip that toe in the water.

Motivation and movement are linked. Get yourself moving. Jump on the spot, jog in a circle, swing your arms about. Notice your elevated heart rate, the new rhythm of your breath – you are alive. What do you want to do with this life? Get motivated. Get living. Sitting around thinking about it won't make it happen. It may help with a strategy but to achieve you need to get up and go. The foot at rest meets nothing; the moving foot is bringing you somewhere.

Action
Try something new

Learn to swim, go to a film on your own – enjoy the trepidation, savour the experience. Find joy in the accomplishment.

Cleachtadh a dhéanann maistreacht

Practice makes mastery

—◄—

The more you practise breath control the more you will master self-control. The more you do those yoga asanas or follow the sutras the quicker you will master them. As an infant, how many attempts did it take to say your first word? How many attempts to stand, to walk, to master holding a cup or using a spoon? We have learned everything we know by repetition. We programme our muscle memory and our thought processes by repetition. Repeated mindfulness will bring about ultimate mindfulness. You can master your destiny – with practice.

Action
Practise

Practise patience. Practise compassion. Practise being you. Practise being in the moment. Practise your practices (prayer, yoga, meditation, mindful washing of the dishes).

Cleachtadh a dhéanann maistreacht

Experience makes mastery

--◄--

Many of the seanfhocail can be interpreted in different ways, which provides not just a richness or diversity of experience, but an involvement with perception changes. Perception changes are the backbone of Jesus' sayings and parables – they train us to not just think about something differently but to action a change in ourselves too.

Here, the Irish word 'cleachtadh', which means 'practice', can also be understood as 'experience' – and yes, practice provides experience (even peak experience) but we can also contemplate how experience brings mastery. Practice is all well and good (and it is well and good) but experience is beyond muscle memory. It is *living* mindfully. The experience is the life of it, the life in it, the living element. When thoughts become feelings, that's when they become real; when you move from thinking you are sad to feeling the sadness, when you move from thinking you are at peace to experiencing peace. Mindful experience can deliver the positive intent and help rein back the negative inclination.

We can also look at experience as the awareness and understanding of the process – the 'total experience', not just the occurrence but its reverberations. A pebble thrown in a still pool makes ripples on the surface and as it sinks through the body of water it ultimately settles into the bed beneath. The calm serenity of being a pebble, settling into the bed of a stream or pool is a metaphor for mindful meditation – we sink down and settle into our resting position. The stream of life can flow by at whatever speed it chooses – we are situated, solid and grounded. But the pebble has generated ripples too. It has imparted or exchanged energy in the process of finding peace at the bed of the pool or stream. Those ripples are no bad thing. We announced our intent earlier in this book by clapping aloud, making reverberations – sound ripples and intention ripples. Our mindful actions also ripple into the world. Our experience impacts the reality we inhabit and the more we practise the more we feel those positive reverberations and we set the vibrational frequency of our world to positivity. Being compassionate makes a compassionate world. Being makes reality.

Action
Explore peak experience

Firstly, read up a little on peak experience by visiting a library or bookstore, or, if you must, use a search engine. You don't have to do an in-depth study, just find out what is meant by the term and how the experience manifests. This is not homework – it is about how taking action is a further commitment to energising your life and mind. Exploring peak experience through a secondary source will validate it in your analytical mind, and you can now completely 'know' that it exists. Write down some examples of peak experience in your life. It may be a workout high, having met a deadline, a buzz from a hobby, a flush of date-night anticipation or a post-coital or post-meditation glow. All such moments are proof of your capacity to experience peak experience and to seek out and register more. Remembering and taking note of your previous experiences and appreciating new ones triggers more frequent occurrences.

Is minic a bhí cú mall sona
A slow hound was often lucky

Pace is not always a marker of success. We are not rushing anywhere. We are transforming the entirety of our life. That's all of our life as we live it – in real time. Mindfulness is not a gym workout to get perfect abs for the summer. There is no panic to achieve. Achievement is the continual doing, whether you are a slow hound or fast hare. Luck is more than chance – it is positive energy, it is a manifestation of abundance, it is feeling the joyous reward of living. Be yourself and be lucky.

Exercise
Slow down

Today or over the next few days take the opportunity to slow down. This is not to stop doing, this is to do with deliberate determination. The modern world is all about speed and instant responses. It is good to step off the treadmill and go for a pleasant stroll. It is good to taste your food rather than just swallow it. It is good to be present in the events and everydayness of your life.

So just make a conscious decision not to rush through everything. Do a task slowly, attentively – this is mindful practice, yes, but don't worry about that, just go slow. Slowing down on a task, journey or decision is a way to hone the skill of accepting calmness. So many are scared or anxious in moments of serenity that it makes meditation and other mindful practices difficult, but taking five extra minutes in the shower or fifteen extra minutes to enjoy lunch are increments to success in mindful living.

Is maith an t-annlann an t-ocras

Hunger is the best sauce

Hunger makes food taste good. There is no fussiness with hunger. When hunger is present everything hits the spot.

Mindful eating is about the connection with your food, with the goodness of it, the aroma, the taste sensation, the vibrancy of the colours, the feel of the textures, the nutrition within – eating is one of the essential experiences of life.

Take the time to slow down the process. Look at the meal, really see it. Its simplicity or its elegance. Appreciate the colour and texture before it hits your palate unnoticed. Let its aroma find you. Anticipate the taste. Take that first bite and savour the experience. Don't rush to gulp – rather, experience the sensations of taste, smell, texture and even temperature – all this data adds to the experience. Eat each mouthful mindfully. Savour it. Enjoy it from moment to moment to moment.

Mindful eating is more than deliberate, conscious eating. It is allowing the full potential of yourself to experience the full potential of the meal – so while we eat and know we are eating, eat and know it is nutritionally restoring us, eat for the pleasure of it, we should also eat for the reality of it. This exercise connects us to the reality of difference, to the diversity of sensation in eating and reminds us how rich the living experience is.

Taste a finger dab of salt – experience it, really taste and acknowledge it. There is no mistaking saltiness. Now taste a finger dab of sugar – experience it – how different it is from salt. Not better, not worse. Different. Taste salt in all its saltiness and sugar in all its sugariness. Now find a range of contrasting items to taste and experience. The task is not to compare them, but to experience their uniqueness. It can be hard to separate honey, sugar and toffee, so by juxtaposing contrasting sensations we can discern the difference without judgement and so find the uniqueness of each.

Expand beyond taste to other sensations. Sip some hot tea, then follow with an ice pop. Have a hard biscuit followed by a soft yoghurt. Experience the taste and sensation of each as if for the first time. We may munch toast for a speedy breakfast and wash it down with coffee, but did we really taste the bread, feel the crunch or the soft warmth where the butter melted? Did we enjoy the chewiness of it? Or was it just ... gone?

This primes the brain to reconnect again with food. Don't think you know what salt tastes like – taste it mindfully and you will really know in that moment. Taste it mindfully next week and you will know it again. Experience it each time.

This is building the capacity to experience life in all its moments.

Exercise
Eat when you are hungry, not when you are bored

Pick a day off when you don't have work to do or any serious decisions to make. Have breakfast, then don't snack or sit around – do what you normally do, and wait. Wait for the hunger to tell you it's time to eat. You may feel something twenty minutes after your breakfast – that's not true hunger, so give it more time. When you get what you think is a hunger pang, wait one hour from that moment and then appraise the situation. Then have something simple to eat, like bread and butter, a yoghurt, a piece of fruit – see how hunger adds sauce. Enjoy this meal; your body has asked for it, and this is part of living. You can refuel and enjoy the process simultaneously. Taste every bite. Be alive in the moment of eating.

Mol gort is ná mol geamhar

Praise the fully grown crop and not the stubble

In this proverb, we may hear the echoes of counting unhatched chickens. However, this is not the pessimist's warning cry, it is more a precautionary tale of waiting – not leaping ahead. The *now* may very well be stubble, so be mindful of that part of this process. Don't try to anticipate ahead – that is the future, not now. The stubble is reality, the stubble is certain, it is where you are, what you have. You can wish it well and extend positive energy for a future crop of abundance, but return to the now and enjoy your crop at its stubble stage. We can rejoice at the harvest, but living for the harvest takes you out of the now – it is a wasted opportunity to enjoy the journey of the seeds you have sown and where they are right now.

There are people who tell you not to get ahead of yourself because they want to keep you in your place.

This proverb is not like those people. Dare to dream, plan to succeed. Do not be limited, but enjoy all stages of the journey. The caution is this: living in the dream of winning the lottery, thinking about it on the commute to work, planning in your mind's eye how to decorate your mansion – all that stops you from asking for a pay rise or upskilling to a better-paid job. You are lost in the warm anticipation, in the fantasy – you need to deal with the reality. When you realise you are ankle-deep in stubble, you can feed it, water it, weed it and get it ready to be an abundant crop. You can nurture it through every stage and bring it to harvest. Then rejoice.

Action
Give thanks to nature with a physical action

Feed or leave out water for the birds, plant some nectar-rich plants for the bees, start a compost heap, pick some litter at a local beauty spot. Give a little of your time to the fullness of life. Whether stubble or fully grown, the crop of nature is worthy of your praise.

Múineann gá seift
Need teaches a plan

—◂—

There is a touch here of the English proverb, 'Necessity is the mother of invention'. But it is not just that need instigates change, it also shows the way to change. Need is the blueprint for change.

Your need to find peace or refine practice brought you to this book, to this page, to this next line. The fact is that realising the need for change is the on switch, and in that split second, change is already happening. Need is not want or desire, nor is it a lack. Need is a catalyst.

Let's just go a little further. Do you need a yoga class this week? Do you need to be extra compassionate today? Do you need to smile right now? Let's journey on. Do you need to drive to work this week or would a walk be better? Do you need all that tinned food in your larder or does a food bank need it more? What don't you need? What do you need? Is there a plan already forming?

Action
List your needs

Finding the now is not about goals, but about living in each moment, fully awake. But being fully awake does not keep the heating on, fully awake does not negate the working week, the holiday break, the events and vicissitudes of life. Some things need your intellect, your hindsight and your future vision. Today is a good day to make a plan of action. What do you need to achieve? How might you achieve it? Create a timetable of steps if you are that sort of person – but acknowledge it and set it in motion today.

Ní fhanann trá le fear mall

An ebb tide does not wait for a slow man

The English-language version that people often equate with this proverb is 'Time and tide wait for no man'. It is true that you have to seize the day and get on with life. Life is in motion; you need to move to be with and of it. It moves without you and won't wait for you. Ask the girl to dance; next week she might have a fiancé. Bring in the harvest today; the frost may hit tomorrow. 'Get on with it' is the message here.

The Irish one, however, notes that being slow is what the ebb tide/life has no patience for. It will move all the quicker for your inaction. It is not so much that life races on – life, like the tide, keeps a regular pace – it is you who perpetrate your own misfortune by being too slow to act. The ebb time has its allotted lifespan; there is plenty of time to cut seaweed or beachcomb while the waters are out, if you set about it. The tide will eventually come in. If you are not maximising the opportunity you will run out of time. The tide will come in before you have finished – for some before they have even started. The chance will be missed if you are busy waiting instead of acting.

Mindfulness hones concentration, hones self-belief, negates daydreaming and second guessing. Slowing down at the appropriate times helps you speed up at the appropriate times.

Don't be slow about grasping opportunities in life. Act now. Grasp life now. Get help now. Make that decision now. Come into the now.

Action
Get busy

Firstly, make a to-do list of three things you *want* to do – not *need* to do. This is a treat list – have a lie-in, bake a cake, take a bubble bath, go to a gallery, get a foot massage. As you make the list, think for a moment about how each one of these would make you feel. Imagine yourself snuggled in bed, sense yourself warm and tensionless in the bath, picture yourself taking that perfect cake out of the oven. Why wait for those good sensations? Tick at least two of them off that list this week.

Secondly, make a to-*be* list with three locations that you can visit this week – a woodland, a city street, a coffee shop. Make attainable choices as you are going to visit them for real in the next seven days. When you get there, consciously observe and follow your breath for a time. Then, return your attention to the pace or energy of the place, be it a tranquil woodland or noisy coffee shop, and practise a minute of meditation in that place. This exercise is about practising 'being' in any place. Mindfulness is not dependent on location – it is not just the local community hall, it is a rush-hour traffic jam and an airport departure lounge too. Mindfulness cannot wait for quiet and perfect scenarios. You must be able to enter mindfulness even in the busiest places even with the busiest schedule.

Tuar an t-ádh agus tiocfaidh sé

Predict good fortune and it will come

～

Just as we previously learned to put bad luck at the bottom of the list, so too we can put good luck at the top of the agenda.

This seanfhocal says fortune/fate is a self-fulfilling prophesy. Envisage it as good and it will come good. Start as you mean to go on. Intent can manifest destiny, intent can summon good fortune. Visualisation can manifest abundance.

If you wake up thinking this is going to be a terrible day, you are setting your brain to scan for all the negative things, and you collate the information to make the day appear terrible. Because you are still dwelling on the burnt toast you fail to hear the birdsong, fail to register the smile of a passer-by, fail to notice the sun is shining, fail to put your hand out for the bus – now you're late and it's a terrible day. You enabled it. Had you been mindful and not mind full of burnt toast, the birdsong might have lifted your mood, the smile may have caused you to smile back and you would have seen your bus approaching. Now, you are at school or work and you have switched off your interest in the rest of the day, because you have justified it and programmed yourself to believe it.

If you wake up thinking this is a great day, the toast may still burn but it is a very minor setback instead of an arrow through the heart. Maybe it's an opportunity to leave early and grab a bagel on the way to your destination or stroll to a nice café for a breakfast treat – soak up a little warmth from the sun and share a smile or two – already the day is getting better. Fortune can be about choices. It is how you see the world, how you choose to react or respond to it.

Exercise

Accentuate the positive

This is one for the start of your day, so if you need to, hold off and do it first thing tomorrow. Before you get out of bed, do the following. Visualise having a shower – feel the warm water on your face and the back of your neck, sense how it refreshes, feel the soothing heat – acknowledge that this eases tensions. Now visualise yourself having a good breakfast – your favourite cereal, a delicious glass of cold juice – acknowledge the good this does you. Now picture yourself having a good day – see yourself smiling, getting things done – acknowledge that this is a productive and pleasant day. Enjoy the fantasy.

Now, get up and have a warm shower – feel the warm water on your face and the back of your neck, sense how it refreshes, feel the soothing heat – acknowledge that this eases tensions. Go have that breakfast of champions. Go have a great day.

Is do áibill fhásas breo
From a spark groweth a blaze

Wow, we are getting Pentecostal now! From that first spark of faith comes a fire that blazes. But it should be one that radiates light, not one that consumes the host – don't burn out on spiritual zeal. This proverb is an opportunity to reflect – are you lost in the fever and thus burning up rather than lighting the world? The fevered fight 'holy wars' and justify torture and other human evils. The fevered are not with God, they are too lost in the fire. You don't have to kill or maim to be a religious zealot – you can do it by condoning or condemning, or by feeling superior on your journey. Having a spiritual ego and religious zeal are not a million miles apart. No matter how far you have come from spark to blaze, you are no more special than your neighbour still striking the flint. There is no ranking – we are all particles in the light of God.

The enthusiastic message of this proverb is to persevere – from that humble and tentative spark, a mighty blaze will grow. The intent will become manifest and manifold. Each meditation, each mindful exercise, each expression of compassion is a strike of the flint, a fanning of the flame, a stoking of the beacon fires. Be assured you are doing right. No need for fever – we have real heat to generate, real waves to make.

Exercise
Hot hands

Vigorously rub your hands together and feel the heat mounting. The energy of friction is warm. Friction is not always a negative. Here it brings heat, great for a cold morning. You have done this many times in your life – often automatically, sometimes consciously.

In reality, when you vigorously rub your hands together you are temporarily and in a minor way friction-burning your hands – but you perceive it as generating heat, not doing harm. Perception is reality, even if reality is interpreting a friction burn as heat. We shape and forge our own perceptions and our own reality. We can transform.

The hand-clap exercise awakens and announces presence. A hand rub can spark the heat needed to make a change. Some people rub their hands with glee. If you are stalling, hesitant, fearful or doubting of tasks to be accomplished, a warm-up is physical proof of the ability that exists within you to make change. Cold hands to hot hands in seconds. Thoughts can change just as quickly.

Bíonn an rath i mbun na ronna
There is luck in sharing a thing

Indeed, there is luck in sharing, but we must understand what luck is. In the Irish psyche, luck is good fortune, the positive energy of the day, the cultivation of goodwill. Yes, the cultivation of goodwill – the manifestation of grace and the participation in life beyond your own thoughts and motivations. Sharing opens the world, brings you into contact with otherness, with 'separateness' from your individual self – uncoupled from personal concern, you can join the world.

For some, the mindful path can be all breath and no real life – breathing is key, breathing is a key, but living opens the door. We can get lost on the path and be removed from the physical world behind our spiritual shield. Keeping some distance and retreating from the mayhem is no harm, but don't absent yourself from life altogether. Sharing is communion – it is communication with the interrelatedness of all life.

There is more to life than the *anapanasati sutta* – mindfulness brings you into contact with the energies and reality of your living spiritual self, but that self is not in isolation from every other self on the planet. Share some breath in that direction – there is luck in it.

Luck and chance are esteemed in Eastern philosophies, but in the analytical West, luck is often seen as superstition. Far from it: the luck in this proverb is the manifestation of grace through compassion, through generosity of spirit, through sharing.

In the Irish psyche, luck is fortune, and fortune is abundance. We reap reward not just by harvesting, but by sharing. This is evident in our ancient Brehon Laws, which were an indigenous system of law developed from pre-Celtic and Celtic customs and passed on orally from one generation to the next. The Bech Bretha (Bee Judgments) were a set of laws governing the keeping of bees and also the distribution of their bounty. What they show is the importance of sharing in establishing and maintaining communal cohesion. The following serve as a sample and example:

If a person found, tended or harvested a swarm in a *faithche* (a small green area belonging to a house or family) then one-fourth of the produce at the end of a year was due to the finder/tender with the remaining three-fourths due to the owner of the house.

If the swarm was found/nurtured in waste land or a location that was the common property of the tribe, then the finder/tender had rightful ownership of the bees and their honey but should pay a dividend of one-ninth to the chief of the tribe.

In other situations, or where bee ownership was established by a single beekeeper, the share was enshrined as follows. Because bees gather their honey from the surrounding locality, the owners of the four adjacent farms have contributed to the harvestable portion and so are entitled to receive a small amount of the honey. The Bech Bretha go on to recommend that if beekeeping is ongoing in a district, then after the third year of production each of the surrounding farms should be gifted or could claim entitlement to a share of the swarm to start their own hive.

Bees and humans are both ultra-sociable and share the ability/desire to live in communities and be altruistic. Share yourself – participate with people. The monk in silence, the hermit in solitude, the guru in seclusion, the greedy beekeeper – all these advance little but selfishness.

Action
Share yourself with others

Share a joke or a smile or a good story today. There is luck in it. Invite friends over and share a meal and good times. Share some of yourself with others – there is all the luck in the world in that.

Dein maith i n-aghaidh an uilc
Do good in return for evil

~<~

We often react rather than respond. Sometimes we react with like for like. Avoiding the cycle of violence, spite or hate is not easy in an epoch of wars and social injustice. The world can seem dark sometimes. But this seanfhocal shows the path out of that – do good, not just instead of evil, but in return for evil.

When you bang your elbow or knee, you instinctively rub it. Why do you do that? What your brain knows is that the sensation of pleasure – the gentle rub – can mask the painful throb of the banged limb. Rubbing the site also flushes it with blood and all the natural healing agents in your bloodstream. Rubbing the sore point generates not only relief at the site but also helps to flood or fool the brain with pleasure signals. We can see from this automatic response that fighting negativity with positivity is instinctual on the physical plane. The trick is in allowing that to happen on the psychological and the spiritual planes.

The psychological self may need retraining to accomplish this (through mindfulness and cognitive therapy) while the spiritual plane just needs the noise filtered out – you don't have to earn God's grace or forgiveness, just be open to it. You don't have to repent for ever; repentance is acceptance of your sin – a split-second admission and moment of clarity. Repentance is also reparation to the sinned against, which is not always so easy. But even if your attempts are shunned, you can acknowledge the pain you have caused and not just express your regret to the universe but extend positivity and compassion to the wounded party. Put it out there, as many times as you need to feel you have sent enough goodwill, then move on. Dedicate your life to compassion and healing. Foster goodwill and live a positive life for the benefit of all humanity. Don't do it as a prison sentence or path to forgiveness – that's not the point. We are all interconnected, and doing good obliterates bad. Doing good is not about topping up karma – doing good is how you live in mindfulness.

If you are the wounded party, and you can't take an apology or none is forthcoming, it doesn't stop you acknowledging your pain and letting go of it. It doesn't stop you uncoupling from the perpetrator, through forgiveness or just by wishing them self-awareness and removing them from your thoughts and considerations. Forgiveness is often seen as a selfless act, but really it is self-preservation.

Revenge is soul-destroying, and it just brings more hate, mistrust, violence, pain and suffering into the world – into your own life. Studies show that revenge can undermine your physical and mental health and that the act of forgiveness can boost your threshold for physical pain, decrease mental anguish, boost immune function and create a sense of wellbeing. Holding a grudge holds you in negativity and undermines your full potential and your optimum health. You can learn more about forgiveness in the Further Reading section at the back of this book.

In order to let go you must acknowledge your anger then choose to not let it define you, accept that stopping the hurt starts now. Make a decision to let go of your anger and any negative thoughts you have about the perpetrator. They will have no hold over you. And letting them go is a positive move. Your anger and animosity link you to that person. Sever that link. A life well lived is the best revenge. Free yourself from ongoing harm by moving beyond it. Let go and live a good life.

Let good be your natural instinct. It is the better choice not just on a moral level, but also psychologically and physically. Staying on the positive path is hard in the face of assault, intimidation or provocation, but why bring more negativity into the world? You don't have to dedicate your life to making the perpetrator feel better, but you can take the opportunity to do good elsewhere. People who wish me ill I wish well in return. Saboteurs and malice I deal with by doing something positive with friends or family or for myself. I don't default into revenge or payback fantasies – I go generate some good instead.

Exercise
Do good in return for negativity

Wish wellness and positivity to those you have done harm or injustice to. Wish wellness and positivity to those who have done you harm or injustice.

Is ait an mac an saol
Life is strange

⤛

This proverb has come to be utilised in the context of 'such is life' – shit happens, shrug it off – but it is much more. It hits upon the fact that you don't necessarily need to make life conform to understandable, non-confrontational, digestible bites. This is life – strange and random, intriguing and dynamic.

The literal translation of this proverb is 'the life is the strange son'. It reinforces the tendency of the Irish psyche to see life as a living entity – even as a familial bond. Even if it is the strange son, it is still a relationship, a participation, a close connection. Life, or indeed the world (as 'saol' can mean 'world' as well as 'life'), is not outside the door. It is in your very home, it is in the people around you – your son, your family, your DNA. You and life are the same stock. So, strange or not, it is not to be ignored.

I love that in the Irish language, life and world share a word. Life is in the world, and the world is also life. Often, spiritual journeys are seen as a removal of oneself from the world – Jesus in the desert, Krishna with garlands of detachment, the Buddha seeking oblivion in his Bodhi place – but how we integrate our spirituality into this world is how we live in the world. If you are prepared to go barefoot and joyous (or at least self-reliant) into the unknown future, then by all means take your socks off – but if you are not prepared to walk away from the comforts and certainties of the world you inhabit then you need to integrate your spiritual self with the real world.

The world doesn't always have to be the big bad world – it is beautiful, precious, breathtaking, heart-breaking, delightful and terrifying all at the same time – but it is life. Be mindful in the moments when it reveals its beauty and mindful when it reveals its ugliness. You are in it, so be in it, but also be of it – be the change you want to see and let your mindfulness permeate it.

And if you are suddenly enlightened, then don't stop chopping wood or carrying water. Life goes on.

Action
The busy pace

We have done something similar already, but this is to reinforce our potential to be in the reality of the world – and not just manufacture a moment of mindfulness under ideal circumstances.

Walk down a busy high street, visit a busy shopping quarter. Go where people are and bustle is prevalent. Walk about that place mindfully – feel your feet on the ground, notice how you move through the crowd, how your hips move, the position of your arms. Follow your breath and become calm. The fuss is all around you, it is not in you and you are not of it. It is not of your doing. You have control over how you experience this moment.

Slow your breaths. You have all the time in the world. You can exist and even be mindful in this hectic place. You can observe and be detached. You can be unaffected. Extend a moment of loving compassion to the busy people; wish them tranquillity in their lives. Feel your own inner tranquillity and detachment from the bustle. Give gratitude for that. Your mindfulness practises are reaping rewards.

Olc síon an sioc, is fearr sioc ná sneachta agus is fearr sneachta ná síorbháisteach

Frost is bad weather, but frost is better than snow, and snow is better than eternal rain

---

Knowing when we have it good even when it appears to be going bad is one of the most difficult perceptions. Awareness can come into play to let us see the wood for the trees, but sometimes it is only with hindsight. This seanfhocal reminds us that it could always be worse – not in a despairing or morbid way, but to spare us hindsight and backward contemplation.

In the now, frost is frost and rain is rain, and it must all be encountered and lived through. Age, gender, background, sexuality, financial status, education – they make no difference. Now is now. You are more than a definition. You are a spiritual being, and more still. Frost or snow on the path, rain or sun on your back, it is all life.

Is fearr mall ná go brách

Better late than never

The greatest tragedy is not that life is short, but that we wait so long to live it. The sin is not lateness, the sin is never attempting to live. It is better late than never.

Action

Just live a little

Not tomorrow, not next week – right now. No more waiting.

Live.

Is giorra cabhair Dé ná an doras

The help of God is closer than the door

—≺—

You are saved. You don't even need to get up and go out of the door. You don't have to journey to God. God is within you.

This is the gospel – the good news – that is buried on page twelve of the newspaper instead of the banner headline. I am not a fan of organised religions, because they tend to fuss over approaching God and make it an ordeal when really it's immediate and natural. With organised religion, the message just tries to get you through their particular door. If this seanfhocal became the prime message, you might not need the smoke and mirrors, or even the spokesperson. You might just live for yourself.

You can keep up with a temple or make religion redundant, that is not important – just know that God is direct. You don't need a designated building, a set of rules or an appointed interpreter. God is with you now. You take God to temple, you don't find God there. And if you find God there, know that God is not left behind when you leave and head for home. God leaves with you.

In your darkest hour, the help of God is closer than the door. Activate your faith, heal thyself and leave the woes of the Pharisees to the Pharisees.

Exercise
Body scan

Find a chair or yoga mat and get comfortable. Relax, close your eyes and breathe normally. Bring awareness to how you are sitting or lying. Feel your body in this posture and how it touches the solidity of the seat or floor. Notice the pressure on your skin and muscles at these touching points. Now focus on your feet and notice the sensations happening there – are they cold, itchy, achy, tense or relaxed? Do not try to modify or adjust them, just recognise and acknowledge the sensation. Move your awareness to your ankles – what is happening there? Now your shins – how do they feel? On to your knees, thighs, buttocks, lower back – register each part and the sensations happening there. Systemically continue to scan your entire body. No dwelling, just noticing. If you drift, simply return to the last part and continue. At the end, rest a moment, follow your breathe, relax, open your eyes and resume your day.

In this exercise, we are sensing each part of our bodies in an individual moment. This is strengthening our capability to be mindful, building the neural networks of focus and acknowledgement in our brains, enhancing the 'non-dwell' command and honing our capacity to return if we drift. Next time you do it, extend wellness to each part of your body.

Níor dhún Dia doras riamh nár oscail Sé ceann eile

God never closed one door without opening another one

By the time Christianity had fully taken hold in Ireland, our proverbs had moved from fortune and luck to the direct intervention of God. God, the universe and fate will not impede your journey. It may appear that the way ahead is barred, but it is one door among many, and there is more than one way through.

If you meet an obstacle, go around, go over, go under or go looking for an alternative route. If you believe in an interventionist God or fate, then you can take this locked door or barred path in your stride – because another one will be provided. And if you don't believe that you are being guided, it doesn't matter – the truth is that there is more than one way to scale a wall.

The great lesson here is not to waste time trying to pick a lock which may not be pickable. Just look around for that other entrance.

Exercise
Lateral thinking challenge

Get a pen and some paper. Draw nine dots in a set of three rows, as below. Without taking the pen off the paper, your challenge is to connect all the dots using only four straight lines. That means one continuous movement with each line starting where the last line finishes and the lines must go through the middle of each dot. This exercise will facilitate thinking outside the box.

●　●　●

●　●　●

●　●　●

Clue: Think outside the box. Go beyond the perceived parameters and use the space beyond 'the box' implied by the dots.

Is binn béal ina thost
A silent mouth is sweet

Need I say more?

Well, perhaps a little more. First, in silence there are no complications or misapprehensions, there is just being. It is good to practise silence. Not every meditation needs to be a chant or audible breath. Not every prayer needs vocalisation. It is mindful to practise nonverbal communication – a smile is as powerful as many words. Smile now to yourself in silence and that smile communicates with God. Putting on a smile and experiencing the silence allows you to perceive a sense of happiness. The smile radiates and is a symbol and generator of happiness – just as you are. How effortlessly the silent smile brings wellbeing to life.

And second, silence crops up a lot in techniques for manifesting spiritual intuition and attentiveness. But do not mistake it for a condition in the contract – the spiritual silence is the stillness of at-oneness. Nothing is needed – it is not a doing, it is being.

This proverb does not advocate that you shut up, that you avoid confrontation, that you refrain from speaking out against injustice, no more than it advocates you halt singing the praises of God. In fact, the construction of this Irish phrase means that it is understood as a temporary silence – just as *tá bron orm* means that sadness is upon you, not in you, not of you – so here the mouth's silence is sweet. Your participation with a silent mouth is sweetness itself, but there is no oath of allegiance to it – it is an experience, and like all experiences it is transitory, returning and renewing but not permanent. If permanent, the taste for it would be less sweet. The Trappist monks who keep vows of silence have bitter beer for company. I do not mean to deprecate their sacrifice, but that always struck me as revealing. I am not about sacrifice. I understand detachment, but suffering in the world does not lessen the suffering of others. I understand 'less', but being joy-less will not save a soul. Silent mouths are sweet, but moving ones should issue sweetness too.

Exercise
Sit in silence

If you meditate or are following the exercises in this book, then you might think that you do this all the time. Job done. But no. This exercise is to sit in silence, not sit silently. Silence is not nothing. Silence is not empty. To know it and reap its reward, we should sit with it from time to time.

Turn off the TV, turn off the radio, turn off your inner dialogue. Wait a moment in that mode. You may suddenly hear the noisy neighbour, the traffic outside or the birdsong – life goes on in your silence. Extend compassion to the neighbour or gratitude to the birds. They are not breaking your silence; they are the fullness of life beyond your silence. Sit with that a while. Consciously hear. Silence is not a perfected state, it is an opportunity for heightened awareness. It is a contribution to yourself – to your self – fully being in the moment-to-moment reality of life. Sit now in that fullness of life and hear the world beyond you. You are in this world and you are in your own state of heightened awareness too – separate but intertwined. At oneness with the self is at oneness with everything.

An rud ná cloiseann an chluas ní chuireann sé buairt ar an gcroí

What the ear does not hear does not worry the heart

When I was a child, I was always making quips and sharing jokes. As a result, an aunt gave me a copy of the epigrams of Oscar Wilde, which was an insight into the power of words and made a deep impression. Around that time – I was about thirteen – I remember a school friend was dying to tell me what somebody had said about me, not out of friendship or even comradery, but simply to stir and take relish in the shit. No matter how much I said I wasn't interested, he kept up with it. It must have been juicy, but I was already bored with small politics and bullshit. I had music, books and older girls to get excited about – who needed the distraction of somebody else's negativity? My final retort was quite Wildean – 'I don't care what anyone says about me as long as they say it behind my back'. I was trying to disarm with humour, but once it came out of my mouth I went on to live with it for many years, even to the present day. I just don't take on board the noise. That's all it is – noise. Good or bad, who cares what people have to say about you? Your life is about your expectations, not the expectations or opinions of others.

So I have a special fondness for this seanfhocal. And it is so relevant to the modern world, which can be full of online conflict, trolls and cyberbullying. Perhaps as a consequence of how the modern world is fuelled by gossip and breaking news, everybody has an opinion and so many express it anonymously or by proxy. A negative comment is just a click away. But who cares – it's all distraction. It's like those old films and cartoons where the devil whispers in a person's ear. The words of distraction want to make you lose your mind – lose your mindfulness. Don't take them on board.

This is not 'ignorance is bliss'. It is too easy for monks and recluses of any faith to disappear up the mountain and into the forest to blank out the world and find God in the silence. It is harder to live in the real world with all its noise and find God or grace or peace there. One way is to filter out the negative. Be concerned about famine or war in the news – and you can give, rally, lobby or boycott – but if it's too much right now for where you are, then skip it. It's not absenting yourself from the world, it is catching your breath for the next fight. It's OK to regroup.

This is more about limiting the distractions that burden the heart. There is more room for true compassion if you ignore and avoid the faux and inane gossip, office politics, bitching and backbiting of those around you. You don't need that noise. Drop that burden, and leave out that worry.

Action
Find a quiet space

Practise 'breathe in, breathe out' – inhale, exhale, find a comfortable rhythm, place your hand on your heart and radiate compassion for the suffering in the world. Now radiate joy to counter that suffering. Love, not worry, must fill the heart.

Cha ghlac dòrn dùinte seobhag
A closed fist won't catch a hawk

To catch a hawk you must lure it in, feed it, befriend it – generally make an effort. This proverb reminds us that intent can be helped along by action. Nothing falls into our laps, nothing worthwhile. So what are you doing to manifest abundance, what are you doing to heighten your self-awareness, what must you do to catch that hawk – and soar with it?

Taking appropriate action is being mindful. Taking action to manifest results and being alert to what action must be taken is also a means and an end. Life is dynamic. Be dynamic. Open your clenched fist and live.

Action

Manifest results

Pick two mindful tools from the start of this book and engage them today – a mindful walk, a seated meditation, expressing gratitude – whatever it is, just do it. Doing can be being. It is not all about relaxed stillness and sweet silence. To live in the world you must live and be active. Be present. Activate mindfulness by doing – that is being. That is being true to yourself and that is the result we want.

Cha ghabhann an dorn druidte seabhac

Empty hands will not lure hawks

This is not just about action and intention, this is about investment. Don't expect without offering. Not all the best things in life are free, and sometimes you may pay as well as pray. Pay for meditation lessons or yoga classes, pay with sacrifices to your social or even family life, pay with your time. You are not paying for the reward, you are exchanging energy as part of your participation with life. All life is an energy exchange, every breath of your life, every reaction within every cell of your body. Think of the food we take from the earth and how we feed the soil upon death. Your exhale feeds the trees, their exhale lets you breathe.

Exercise
Exchange energy with a tree

There is no harm in hugging the odd tree – it is good to release gratitude into the world. Whether you hug or not, find a tree and meditate beneath it. Follow your breath in gratitude to the synergy between human and nature. You and this tree are replenishing each other, are alive together. In your mindful sharing of existence, there is union with God. Remember, the Buddha found *nirvana* beneath a tree. For now, gratitude and connection is enough. Your hands are no longer empty.

Ma's fada a bhios an t-ágh, thig se fa dehireadh

Though luck may be long in coming, it comes at last

On one level, this proverb is about perseverance. If you can wait long enough, be steadfast, then things will change. Whether in circumstances or perception, a change will come, and things will get or appear better. Sometimes distance or time is the healer, and what was a problem, pressure or embarrassment yesterday will be minor next week and nothing at all next month. Hang on. It gets better. This is brilliant wisdom. Do not waste time on despair – have confidence in change, in the evolution of the situation, in your ability to move beyond the circumstances.

On another level, this proverb says don't worry. You need not put effort in to being resilient and steadfast, because it will happen for you. You don't need to dwell on how poor or bad your current luck is, because it's going to change automatically. That frees you up to live and to be truly mindful. You can be mindful in this moment and not have to focus on how good or bad your luck is – your luck or grace or status make no difference. Now is for now, tomorrow will look after itself.

> **Exercise**
> Greetings from happiness
>
> Get some paper, colouring pens and even glitter. Fashion a postcard that says 'greeting from happiness'. Be as creative as you wish – from a simple smiley face to a beautiful collage of magazine cut-outs. When complete, address it to yourself and write a nice greeting from this happy place – a positive message. Now put it in your mailbox, in your hallway or on the fridge – somewhere you will find it tomorrow. Go to bed, sleep, dream, forget. Tomorrow you will find this postcard and it will be a portent of happiness – a reminder to be happy, to seek happiness, to think of your 'self' as being happy.
>
> By doing this exercise you show loving compassion and extend positivity to yourself. Affirmations like this are immediate good will and good energy.

Alius a mhaoile féin do loisgeann gach éinne

The sweat of one's own brow is what burns everyone

We feel our own pain the most, but we are not alone in experiencing pain. This is a reminder to not get too caught up in our troubles or exertions – everybody has to live through pain and suffering.

Pain and suffering can teach us to have compassion for others and also for ourselves – so it is not always a bad thing.

Exercise
Show compassion in response to pain

Show compassion and empathy to somebody who is telling you their woes – even if it's only a litany of first-world problems. Exercise compassion towards your own self when next in pain, but don't let it consume you – that's just self-pity.

Maireann croí éadrom i bhfad

A light heart lives a long time

This is the 'don't worry – be happy' proverb, but it is not saying to abandon intellectual engagement, concern or compassion and become blasé and trivial. It is simply acknowledging the fact that not only does stress kill, but happiness lengthens your life. Laying burdens down and not picking up more tiny and unnecessary concerns is beneficial to health and longevity. Bringing more joy and peace into your heart will lengthen your life.

Stress is the body's automatic reaction to harmful situations – be that situation real or perceived. Sometimes, the perceived or mental situations seem to carry more jeopardy than the real physical threats. Some behavioural psychologists argue that we evolved this mechanism as an early warning survival system, so that the sound of the breaking twig (which may be the approach of a predator or just a family member) triggers a flight or fight response in preparation for the appearance of the sound maker and the possibility of attack. We all have different fears and triggers, but we all have the same inbuilt reaction, and that starts in advance of having the full facts.

When you feel threatened, this 'fight or flight', reaction is automatically switched on. It is a chemical reaction that quickens your heartbeat, increases your respiration, tightens your muscles and pumps some adrenalin into the system. The aim is to get you dramatically alert – you are prepped and pumped, there is no mistaking this for a dream, you are switched on, you are not caught off guard. You are ready to hit back – fight – or you have the capacity to sprint as fast as you can in the other direction – flight. It doesn't matter what decision you take, your whole body has been activated towards possible survival.

The problem is that not every perceived threat turns out to be real, so we don't get to punch it in the face and release the pumped-up aggression or burn off the nervous tension with a rapid retreat. We are left with all this 'surge' and nowhere to release it. Shouting at your email, road rage, January sales aggression, panic attacks, etc. are all symptoms of this fight or flight response. Fearing the worst after a medical test or fretting you have failed your exams is the same thing – the chemical reaction is activated every time you mentally revisit the worst-case scenario. Mindfulness can earth that electrical charge and bring you back into control.

Stress was an evolutionary advantage that we didn't drop. We still need it, but the problem is we engage it when faced with non-life-threatening events – low phone battery, running out of milk, shoes not matching belt. We need to disarm it when it's not really required and save it for the real zombie apocalypse, the escaped tiger, the mugger – and not virtual versions of those scenarios or petty office politics. Repeated or prolonged exposure to stress and its body-altering consequences can cause real physical problems, including aches and pains, teeth grinding, headaches, nausea, insomnia, high blood pressure, self-esteem issues and a higher risk of depression.

Happiness means different things to different people. It is a state of mind, a self-perception – some achieve it with a positive evaluation of their life, some by redefining their expectations of success, some by carefree living, some have their work/life balance in check, others believe it is simply their innate disposition. For certain, we can say that happiness is not an equation and is difficult to measure, but we can all acknowledge that it is easy to recognise. You can't miss happiness when you see it in others – it shines through. It permeates their whole being.

Happiness is a positive emotion. If you are experiencing it, then you are not experiencing negative emotions (which have proven health implications). Happiness generates a sense of wellbeing as well as interrupting sensations of non-wellbeing. It triggers not just psychological but also physiological wellness. Feeling happy decreases awareness of pain and also facilitates stronger antibody responses, thus boosting your immune system and further sustaining wellness. Having a laugh, smiling more, doing activities that bring you satisfaction or joy are all life-extension tools. I am not just saying it, many studies show a link between happiness and longevity. You can read more about happiness in the Further Reading section.

Life is short but is too long to be miserable in. A burdened heart gets less joy from life, gets jaded quicker and loses the will to live or fight illness when it comes.

Exercise
Smile and laugh

It doesn't have to be to anybody, it doesn't even have to be to yourself in a mirror. Just put a smile on your face for thirty seconds. Notice how it makes you want to smile for real. Think of a fond memory or loved one, and go with it. Truly smile. Make a silent vow to smile more often.

Now, try laughing. You don't have to force this one. You may laugh all the time at work, with friends and so on, but this exercise is about noticing the sensation, not the punchline. Simply take some time out to watch a funny film. Or select a show that you know always makes you laugh. Watch as you would normally – don't anticipate, just watch. When laughs happen, notice your sense of wellbeing. Don't try to exaggerate the laugh. Just enjoy the ones that arise, feel how they do you good. Acknowledge and enjoy them.

Ag duine féin is fearr fhois cá luigheann a bhróg air

The wearer of the shoe knows best where it pinches

Trust your own experiences. You know what is right for you. You have instincts; you get bad feelings about things, and you get adrenalin surges when it's time to play that match or stare down that growling stray dog. Our instinct is an early warning system. Our gut reactions are not clouded by analytical thought processes, they are immediate reactions. Trust, trust, trust.

Action

Find where the shoe pinches

Make a list of where your shoe pinches, and over the coming weeks and months, make time to rectify these sore spots.

Mairg do ní deimhin dá bharamhail

Woe to him who deems his opinions a certainty

Yes, woe to him indeed. You are setting yourself up for a fall if you attach yourself to opinionated stances. This does not mean you should waiver in your convictions, relinquish fundamental truths or abandon values – no, this speaks to me of the trap of mastery. Yes, practice brings mastery, but this is mastery over breath control, over mind wandering, over your thought-to-feeling processes – not mastery over the supposedly 'lesser enlightened'. Don't confuse the path to enlightenment with the notion of a social hierarchy, and don't mistake enlightenment for a culmination of civilisation. Ignore the man-made 'religions' – there is no hierarchy in oneness, it is all-encompassing.

The concept of the sinner, of the unawakened, of the lower caste is not enlightened. It is nothing but a manufactured pretext to gain power or rank or status. Many people on the journey we are sharing through this book may have awoken to the misogynistic, homophobic, capitalist and always power-seeking stance of organised religion and have decided to shun it. Some will have shunned the one they grew up in and picked up a new religion – but thinking you have escaped the evil in Christianity for the good in Islam or Buddhism (or indeed vice versa) is choosing to ignore the corruption and evils in the newly adopted faith. A zealot is a zealot in any faith – misogyny, homophobia, wealth alliances and power-seeking stances are wrong in any faith or any branch of organised religion. Those certain opinions are woeful. If God weeps, God weeps at that.

Some on the journey abandon all faiths for their own faith, perhaps cherry-picking a little from many spiritual systems, but obey no doctrine. That may be my own personal story, my own particular pathway, but the *tao* of myself is the *tao* of myself – it is not superior to the *tao* of yourself. I may pontificate a bit and lay out some insights and even opinions in this book, but I am asking you to consider and take your own actions – not replicate mine. The aim is to break from opinions and live. Not to create a whole new set. Obey yourself, not others. Obey yourself, do not order others. Some on the journey make the mistake of thinking they have mastered it and it is their right or duty to let everybody know – or worse, help everybody conform to the way they have found. Woe to him who deems his opinions a certainty.

Exercise
Enter the unknown

Today, do something you have never done before. Perhaps don't streak at a televised sports event, but maybe you could roller skate around the local park, have a vegan meal, go to a jazz club or buy some flowers for a stranger. Feel the trepidation and embrace the fear of foolishness – it is only a moment. It is just a task.

Sense the acknowledgement of unease, of uncertainty. Then, once you have done it, sense the triumph of accomplishment. You may have found out that you don't like jazz, you may now wonder how you ever lived without roller skates. The unknown is soon known. New experiences break fixed patterns.

Seachain droch-comhluadar
Shun evil company

Far from moralising, this is in your best interest. We can take evil to mean bad and bad to mean negative. Avoid those preoccupied with darkness, gloom, misery, greed, anger, violence and vices that impede the joyful life. You are not passing judgement on the ways of others, you are just with the *tao* of positivity now.

Jesus may have sat with the sinners. You don't have to. You are not even to make judgements on who is a sinner, you are just parting company with the potential to sin. Peer pressure doesn't necessarily stop after the teenage years. You know who diverts you from your full potential. Lessen and cease if possible your exposure to them or radically change your reactions when in their presence. The word 'evil' may seem extreme – but whatever is stopping you having a full life is as dangerous as evil. They could be the friends that get you drunk and let you make mistakes or the moralising ones who make you feel bad for wanting to dance or wear your hair a certain way. The preachers who control morality can be as dangerous and unhelpful as the devils on your shoulder egging you on.

Shun evil company and live a good life for yourself.

Exercise
Guilt-free breaking away

For all sorts of reasons, we can accumulate people who are not good for us but are hard to walk away from. It may be an ex, an old friend who hasn't moved along with your life changes, or it may be a psychic one – a dead relative or someone still living. I am talking about the people who populate our headspace and drain our emotional reserves. You need to break that connection.

Picture an old steam train, like one from an old movie – with a band on the platform, balloons, bunting and flags everywhere. This is the maiden voyage of a once-in-a-lifetime luxury trip – a trip away into happiness and resolution. All the people you need out of your head are here. They are all happy and they have a golden ticket in their hands. They are smiling at you, joyous, laughing – there are no hard feelings, sorrow or pain here. They are winners. You show them onto their carriage, they wave at you out of the window. You blow the whistle and the train departs – they are happy to go, and you are happy to have sent them off. Let them go.

Now they are gone. Feel the relief. Trust that the connection is broken in a beautifully positive way. You wish them well on their journey, and they are happily gone. Live your life now.

Aithnigh cú géur a lócht
A sharp hound knows its faults

You are not perfect. That's OK, that's not what is being asked.

This seanfhocal points out that knowing and acknowledging our faults is the key – the sharp hound knows that. We are flawed, but we function. We can move beyond our faults, we may even work with them. The small and slight hound may sprint faster. We can work with what we have got. Only the arrogant think themselves superior, flawless, blameless – they are the dogs that tumble taking the turn.

As humans, we may obsess about our physical faults, social status or other assumed 'imperfections'. Sometimes we neglect the real flaw – bitterness, greed, envy, spite. But knowing your faults means you can work on them – not to please God, but to improve your life. Faults can hold us back, and recognising the problem is the first step in tackling it. The sharp hound knows that.

Action
Make a personal SWOT analysis

Draw four columns on a page and label them strengths, weaknesses, opportunities and threats. Now begin filling them in. Don't ponder too deeply, just put down what arises in the moment. 'I am motivated' might be a strength or 'I have a good memory'. A weakness might be inconsistency or hesitancy – you know yourself better than anybody so be truthful, no one else will see this list. List some opportunities that could help you flourish – getting a library card or a mindfulness app. Jot down some threats – a busy time at work is approaching, final exams are this year.

Knowing your strengths and weakness is a way to maximise your talents while avoiding pitfalls. Knowing what opportunities or threats are on the horizon can help you steer a steady course and make preparations.

For now this is just to see yourself. It is good to take stock and to face reality, to see how you view yourself truthfully. Of course, you now can also be grateful for your strengths and opportunities and you can start to formulate ways to resolve your weakness and threats.

Is fearr lúbadh ná briseadh
It is better to bend than to break

Pride and stubbornness are not self-respect and determination. Pride and stubbornness can make you inflexible. The man-made straw hut is a construct, the blade of the grass in the field is natural – but come the hurricane the grass will bend and recover, while the solid hut is lashed, battered and blown apart. It is better to bend than to break. It is natural to be flexible. 'Adapt and survive' is not just a saying, it is evidenced by all life on earth – elephants no longer wear fur, the ice age long past, yet they continue to exist.

Flexibility is important. Flexibility is the *tao* of life.

Action
Limber up

Do some stretches, a spot of yoga or Pilates. Feel how it makes you feel. Become aware of the physical changes in your body – the release of tension, the energised self, the loosening of the grip of stress, the revitalised or eased mind. Limbering up before a workout is essential, but physically limbering up before an emotional challenge brings energy and presence to the situation. No harm in doing a few stretches or star jumps before a job interview, an awkward chat with a family member or a counselling session. Just not in the same room.

Is fearr obair ná caint

Work is better than talk

⤙

This may be the mantra of your line manager, but the true meaning is to put up or shut up. Many people talk a good game but don't take action. Intent can set you free, but intent with action definitely will.

Action
Do it

Stop talking about losing weight and getting fit – do it.

Stop talking about volunteering time to a good cause – do it.

Stop talking about all your plans – put them into action.

Work and action are better than talk and procrastination – do something for yourself.

Get to work.

Is fearr muinighin mhaith na droch-aigneadh

Good hope is better than bad intention

Not everything in life is black or white. We hope to live a virtuous life, we hope to walk in the light, to shun evil deeds and thoughts – but we must accept our failures in that regard too. Be mindful of darker emotions and thoughts. We don't have to indulge them, but Buddha didn't get fat by avoiding the temptation of good food. That does not mean he indulged greed, just that the moderation he preached was not as easy to practise. But that's OK, because good hope is better than bad intention. You don't have to be perfect to find *nirvana*.

Exercise
Good hope meditation

Sit or lie down and begin with about thirty seconds of following your breath. Now think of your hopes – hopes for yourself, hopes for others. Just recount them in your mind, no need to dwell on them. Now follow your normal meditation practices to enter a state of serenity. From this serenity, bring your awareness to the state of calm that exists within you – this is good energy, this is positive energy. Extend it as good hope into the world. Let it radiate from you. There is joy in this. You may smile, you feel good – extend this joy and goodness into the world. It may last a moment or it may last the duration of your meditation, but the good hope is sent. Its ripple will be felt.

An té a thabharfas scéal chugat tabharfaidh sé dhá scéal uait

The person who brings you a story will also bring two away from you

---

This seanfhocal teaches us how to deal with gossips. My mother and all her side of the family would often say 'there's nothing worse than a story carrier'. There are worse things – but we often excuse the subtle evils. 'Evil' sounds like a harsh word, but spreading stories, be they lies or truth, perpetuates the pain of the real-life characters in the story. Telling tales keeps the misery or embarrassment energised. Don't participate in that. Radiate joy and compassion, not squalid fervour.

The lesson to be learned in this seanfhocal is that these gossip-mongers don't just spread it about others – they spread it about you too. Give them no time and you deprive them of the oxygen needed for their pernicious actions. Be wary of the tattletales – they have self-esteem issues and they are dangerous.

They will not only spill your beans, but they will season and garnish the meal too. If you are a gossip, drop it now. Life is short but it is too long for constant misery and ill will.

Funnily enough, before gossip meant 'idle talk' it evoked a close confidant. A *godsibb* was a sort of proxy for God, such as a godfather or godmother – someone with whom you could commune. But it soon devolved from sharing the intellectual manifestations of divine participation into the worst sort of nonsense, just as the gospel moved from the 'good news' of all that is right into the misery of sin. There is only one sin – intent with malice. It may manifest as murder or rape, but it can also manifest as spite and gossip. Don't underestimate the cumulative effect of small actions. Don't magnetise your mind, body and spirit to the repetitive and retentive smallness of spite and gossip.

Action

Meet gossip with good news

Reclaim the good intention of godsibb and gospel. Give a story of light to stop the one of darkness being told. It doesn't have to be about the glory of God – all this rain has my lawn looking so green, did you hear so-and-so passed their driving test – that is also the glory of God. Positivity is the way. Every moment of every day.

If you are the gossip, tell a good story or share a positive fact to a random stranger every day for two weeks. Not random acts of kindness to give you an endorphin hit for doing good, but a deliberate communing with positive intent. It's that simple.

Bád gan stíuir no cú gan eireaball

Boat without a rudder or dog without a tail

Direction. Mindfulness delivers direction. Mindfulness is a tool in a world where we seem to be headless chickens, rudderless boats and tailless dogs, reacting to everything and not responding to anything. Mindfulness will help you navigate the spiritual path and the hectic days equally well.

Exercise
A planned walk

Plot a route from your house to a friend's or from work to home. Think of the best way to get there – either the quickest or the most scenic route, whichever you fancy. Visualize waking it, every turn and landmark you will pass. Later in the day, do the same journey in your mind again. Later on, do the journey for real and actually walk it.

In this you have successfully accomplished a plan of action. You had a rudder – intent. You also had the wind in your sails – motivation. Planning routes is a workout for the hypothalamus – that part of your brain that maintains homeostasis and gives direction to your endocrine and nervous systems. It is interesting to note that taxi drivers have an enlarged hypothalamus, while drivers reliant on Sat Nav or fixed routes tend to have average to below average ones.

Ní bhíonn an rath, ach mar a mbíonn an smacht

There is no prosperity unless there is discipline

—≺—

So we are some way through the book now. It is timely to ask how you are doing. Have you found your flow? Are you in the zone? Is there the discipline of practice? Are you noticing the reward?

There is no prosperity without discipline. Without discipline, without continual engagement with mindful living, without regularly practised exercises, there is no attainment.

Mindfulness is not a hobby you do every Friday evening. Without regular attention to it, it becomes a pastime instead of a life choice. So do you have the discipline to get to yoga once a week? Can you take a break from work to see the beauty of a sunrise? Can you find awe in the leaves in the trees or the birds in the air?

Do you have the discipline to wash the dishes mindfully, to make love mindfully, to meet the world mindfully?

Action

Reflect on your progress

Meditate for few minutes and notice how good you have become at catching the drifting. You have come far from following a few breaths at the beginning of this book. Continue on course.

Ná bris do loirgín ar stól nach bhfuil i do shlí

Do not break your shin on a stool that is not in your way

Don't go looking for trouble. There is no need to go out of your way to complicate your life any more than it already is. Too often we set up hurdles that we don't need. I will learn to cook in the New Year after I get fit. Worse – I will get fit after I learn a new language, move to that country and join a gym there. Worse again – I will become a compassionate person when the world respects me.

Walk a straight path. It's so much easier. Walk a straight path and don't fear success, don't slow progress – stop diverting your full potential.

This also applies to unnecessary stresses, which we too often bring upon ourselves – checking the emails before breakfast, answering the phone when we're already late, agreeing to extra when we are already busy. It's about control and about being conscious. If you were truly present, you would not be stumbling through life and breaking your shins.

Action

SWOT in action

Return to that SWOT analysis you carried out a few weeks back. Have you worked on any of the weakness that arose? If yes, then keep up the good work. If not, pick one and tackle it. Do a course, get an app, talk to a friend, seek help. Remember the knot at the throat in the second proverb? Don't go through life hampered. Most weaknesses are just fear, so drop the fear. Some are skill deficits that can be remedied. Apply yourself to yourself – this is not selfishness, it is bringing a better self into this world and into the lives of all you encounter. Your full potential is for everyone's benefit. Your full potential might be contagious.

Adeir siad ná deaghaidh fial go hiofrann

They say a generous man has never gone to hell

━━◅

If a generous man has not gone to hell, does one automatically go to heaven? Too often we think of heaven and hell as an afterlife – a consequence of a bad life or the reward for a good life. Really, hell is the life we are living and heaven is the life we could be living.

Forget the afterlife today and be generous to yourself – to your soul, mind, body and spirit. Live a moment of heaven. Buy yourself an ice cream and enjoy every single lick. Kick your shoes off and enjoy the freedom your feet now feel. Do something to awaken and celebrate the joy. Bake yourself a cake, run yourself a bubble bath, smell your favourite flower, press play on your favourite song and sing along with it.

It is OK to love yourself – just don't hoard your love away from everyone else. Treat yourself – the joy, happiness or wellbeing that you will feel is not a selfish thing, it is a radiating thing. It will ripple into the world and into the rest of your day and energise not just you but whoever else you encounter. Smiles are as contagious as yawns. Go generate one for yourself – then share it.

Action
Be generous

This week, be generous with your time (with family, with friends or with colleagues). Perhaps donate some time or money or old books to a charity or leave a nice tip for someone doing you a service. At the end of the week, be generous to yourself – begin a meditation and extend good health and good luck to yourself. This is not a pat on the back, rather this is generating more generosity.

Ná cuir an mhaith ar cáirde

Don't withhold friendship/don't postpone a good deed

Do good in the world. Don't miss those opportunities to be a good friend or to do a good turn for a stranger. Random or premeditated makes no difference – just unleash your full potential through genuine acts of kindness.

Giving should come easy. It's a survival trait from the earliest days of human society. Sharing a living location and being a tribe includes sharing skills, food and resources. We are hardwired to participate in altruistic behaviour to maintain social cohesion within the tribe, within our community. When we act kindly towards another person we are saying we are same, not enemies, and so we create a connection. We also set up the potential for reciprocity.

Within give and take there is no hierarchy, though it may appear so sometimes. Sometimes people forget and think gratitude is subservient to generosity, or generosity is a 'gift' of the privileged to the lesser off. Generosity is not status, it is an intrinsic need. We need to give. We are natural born givers. Giving thanks is as good as giving gifts. Giving time is as good as giving money.

The act of giving actually activates regions of the brain (the mesolimbic pathway, to be precise – which is the reward centre in the brain) associated not just with social connection and trust, but with pleasure. Christmas is a global hit, not for any celebration of Jesus Christ but rather due to the actions of the wise men. Gift giving engenders in the giver a 'warm glow'. Many studies have found that altruistic actions release endorphins in the brain and flood the body with a sense of wellbeing and joy, sometimes referred to as 'helper's high'. Every time you do a favour or a random act of kindness, you get a little hit of pleasant endorphins to validate your action and prime you for repeat actions. That doesn't mean you can get addicted to giving, just that there is a reward in it for you.

Giving is sometimes framed as a moral choice and sold as a spiritual duty. I am with Anthony de Mello, who advocated not doing something for somebody if you expect something in return. Doing good to get into heaven or to feel like a better person is morally bankrupt. Don't get hung up on your 'goodness'. It's not about being good – it's just about being human. Giving and sharing is what we do. If you are being human, your 'being' is in play with others around you. Together we are giving and taking, and together we share ourselves. You can find more about altruism in the Further Reading section at the end of this book.

Exercise
Random acts of kindness

For the next week, do a random act of kindness each day. We often do these, but simply don't notice. Leaving a tip, dropping coins in a charity box, giving a friend a lift or a neighbour a dig out can just be automatic – you may even be sleepwalking through your generosity. This exercise is to acknowledge and accept that you are capable of goodness, mindfully following your inherent altruistic desires. Random acts of kindness are not 'charity' – they are humanity.

Here are some suggestions.

Compliment somebody who gives you good service or does a good job.

Post something nice. Social media can be a mine of self-pity and emotional retaliation. Today, post a compliment or thank you to a friend or colleague.

Post home. Take time to write a letter or postcard to a family member wishing them well.

Put up a positivity noticeboard in the office for all to share their good news. Giving people a chance to not be embarrassed about this is a great kindness.

Bring some treats to work or make a cupcake care package for the staff at your closest hospital or hospice.

Listen – really listen. It can be difficult to not interrupt when someone else is speaking, but today don't jump in with advice – just listen supportively.

Donate some books to the local school, hospital or prison.

Organise a local tidy-up day – and if no one shows up, do what you can anyway.

Add an extra tin of food to your shopping basket each week and make a hamper for a local charity. You could buy dog food if there's a rescue centre nearby.

Nior bhris focal maith fiacail riamh

A kind word never broke a tooth

❧

You have heard of random acts of kindness – how about some random acts of praise?

We often think positively of our loved ones, but do they know how often or even what we think about them? Verbalise those good feelings. Sure, it's a bit awkward to splurt them out without context, but get over that. Say 'I love you' first, not in reply. If you were thinking of somebody earlier, tell them that you were. Let people know – it won't break your teeth.

The same goes for your friends. The same goes for the helpful cashier or the dutiful parking attendant. 'Good job' – how hard is that? 'Thanks a million' – how hard is that? It is not flattery, it is a genuine acknowledgement of the significance of that person in your life or the contribution they have made to your day.

Exercise

Say some nice things today

It's not just nice to be nice. It, like gratitude, altruism and so much of social interaction, is beneficial to our psychological and physiological health – it makes us see the world better and feel better in it. The receiver of the praise is brightened too. There is nothing but good in it. So say nice things to the people you meet today.

Bíonn blás ar an mbeagán
A little can be tasty

—←—

This seanfhocal echoes Buddha's teachings on moderation – that little can be enough, and we don't have to be greedy or gluttonous. In a world of convenience and perpetual calls to consume more – more of everything – it is a timely and perhaps contentions reminder. We do not need a lot to be fulfilled – to have our bellies full or our spirit replenished.

As we sleep we regenerate and repair. During the day we can act and be awake or we can sleepwalk through life dreaming of all that allegedly glitters. How many shoes or shirts do you need? What do you own that will save your soul? What do you really need? A little of what you really need is as tasty and nourishing as the promise of a full plate or a whole banquet of physical acquisitions and psychological procurements.

Overkill is relevant in the spiritual reality too. 'I trust in thee' or 'I trust in me' is enough of a prayer. Taking part in yoga, reiki, meditation, prayer group, temple visits and scripture readings all in one week is just showing off. We may do all these things to top up our sense of purpose or to feel good on the journey, but we should be wary of bringing the consumerist fever to our practices. You cannot get awareness off a shelf. You don't need to trolley dash through all of your life. Moderation is good everywhere – life on earth is for living too.

This seanfhocal lets us know there is great taste in little things, great rewards in little steps. The increments of your path and adjustments to a more mindful life have their own tastes – you don't need to rush to the final meal. Enjoy the fruits foraged along the way.

Exercise
Fast to appreciate

Fast for even half a day and break it with a single bite of your favourite fruit or food – just one little bite – and put the rest away for an hour or so. For now, this exercise is in the taste, texture, fulfilment of that morsel – this is eating in the now. A fuller meal later will bring pleasure, but this bite brings gratitude and a sense of the preciousness of a single bite.

Buadhann an fhoighde ar an gcinneamhain

Patience conquers destiny

All good things come to those who wait. Well, not always – sometimes you have to get up off the couch and go bring the harvest in. But anxiety is the great undoer. It physically hurts us and wounds our psychological health and spiritual wellbeing. Patience, true patience – the steady acceptance that things take time and every season offers new opportunities – is a gift that prolongs life and health, that keeps us on an even keel on spiritual journeys and within the psychological narrative we tell ourselves.

You may have heard that 'patience is a virtue'. Well, it truly is. In this seanfhocal we learn of its power – so powerful is patience that it conquers destiny. But this is not to say you have to live a preordained life. You can escape your circumstances, you can feel better, achieve more. There is no fixed destination. We know change is the breath of life, and we can change our supposed destiny – it is never too late. Sometimes it is through direct action, and sometimes it calls for patience. Having faith in yourself and in the divine energy of the universe or God's love will manifest change and will conquer destiny.

Practising patience is also a spiritual tool to strengthen resolve and to make use of response rather than reaction. Reaction can be kneejerk, but response can be considered and mindful. The crying child may need a hug instead of a sharp word, no matter how busy or stressed you are – responding enables the right actions, reacting lets everybody down. You don't have to hug the driver who cut you off or the colleague with the snide comments – you just don't have to carry that energy with you. You can keep your patience with them and let the negative energy dissipate rather than perpetuate it with a reaction.

Practising patience slows the need to react; it gives a proper pace to your life that makes space for harmony and wellbeing. Who needs an instant reply? The modern world has us all but a text or email away from more concerns, more calls to action, more workload, more gossip, more hassle, more replies, more time-wasting. Power off on your days off – let the business world, social world and family world all learn patience too.

As well as bad drivers, ignorant people and bold children, you can practise patience with your expectations as well. Meditation is patience, prayer is patience, yoga is patience. Sitting in a garden and feeling the sun on your face is not just mindfulness – it is patience. Patience is mindful.

Exercise

Practise patience.

Everything takes time, everything requires attention and focus – everything calls upon your concentration and patience. Now be patient with yourself, with your drift into thoughts, with all your good intentions and all your failings. Be still a moment – be patient. You are getting there.

An rud a théann i bhfad, téann sé i bhfuaire

What drags on only grows cold

Why wait so long? Patience is a virtue, procrastination isn't – there are times when action is required. Your *now* needs attention *now*!

We don't need to make a meal of every change. Letting go or stepping up is a split-second decision – every thought you have is in the firing of synapses in your brain. Think of a light switch – it takes one second to turn it on or off. Think of a teenage love or a hobby that engrossed you as a younger child – how one moment it was everything to you and then you were over it. It may not have been instant, but change happened and you survived. It's the same with finding your inner resolve. One moment you fear what people think of you, the next it doesn't matter a jot. It's the same with doing what you want to do with your life.

This proverb lets us know that if we have to wait a long time for something, it grows cold. The trail can go cold too and we can give up, or when we get there we may have gone off the idea. Don't let your aspiration go cold. Act upon it. Go for it. Take a step closer to your goal.

Action
Don't drag it out

Do not procrastinate; strike while the iron is hot and get the job done. Make that change now. If it seems too big (end the bad marriage, leave the boring job, move away) then make the first move (see a solicitor, look up other jobs, review finances) – the first move is a step closer not just to the change but to your actual full potential.

Even if you have no big life changes to make, you can still take the dynamism of change into you. So make a simple change now.

Declutter your bedroom – bring harmony to not just where you sleep but where you wake and start your day.

Get up earlier and walk to work/college/or your other daily destination – experience the journey and all the life between your home and the end point.

Go see a band/play/film that wouldn't normally be on your radar. Even if you hate it, getting out of your comfort zone is good practice for other occasions.

Buy a different brand of cereal, maybe go vegetarian for a week, or try out the national dish of wherever the pin lands on the map.

Change invigorates perception and self-awareness. Be renewed and stop waiting for cold soup.

Bíonn gach duine go lách go dtéann bó ina gharraí

Everybody is good-natured until a cow goes into their garden

You are nearing the end of this book and have a great deal of exercises and actions behind you – so it is time to look at the difficult truth of this seanfhocal. The real test of one's character only comes in times of adversity. You may be on a spiritual high or feeling grounded and in control, and then all of a sudden something shocking or detrimental happens. Don't be set back by it – life happens, we move on and let more life happen – don't get caught up in the disasters and crises that occasionally befall us, and if you don't react in a considered and mindful way, don't beat yourself up over it. You are human too – the spiritual path is not about killing emotion. You may come to temper anger and not switch on regret, but without experiencing emotions from time to time we are but machines.

Life circumstances shape us, and if you have experienced enough flak in your life, you either crack at the first shot or you are cool and composed under fire. If you have never been tested, it's anybody's call. How you respond – not react – to adversity is part of the path. It is not about being exclusively good. Letting an expletive fall from your mouth is not a ticket to hell – it's what honestly happened in that moment. Sainthood does not mean abandoning anger at injustice; however, feeling sorry for oneself is not a valid sense of injustice.

Maybe you are at a place where you can calmly stroke the brow of the cow, lead it home and then return and replant your garden without consternation. You will live longer if you are there. You will have an easier path through the adversities to come if you are there. But if you are not there, take each failure to be cool, calm and objective as a chance to be aware of the need to practise more compassion and understanding. Take each opportunity to engage with patience and understand that random mishaps are not the malice of the universe or even the fault of the cow – or even yourself if you happen to have left the gate open.

Good nature is sometimes hard work. Good nature is sometimes naturally present without effort. When we learn to take the opportunity to utilise the mishap as an opportunity to replant the garden a different way, then goodness will prevail and prosper.

Action

Fix the gate

Being in the now does not preclude you from considering the future from time to time and preparing for potential situations. Are there gates to be fixed? Cows to be soothed?

Caitheann síor-shileadh an chlioch

Continuous weathering wears the rock

Some things take time, such as being mindful in company, transcending the conditioning of a lifetime and so on. But the outcome is inevitable. This proverb reminds us of that – perseverance leads to success.

Each day that you practise mindfulness or proceed in awareness, you erode the old conditioned self and you shape a new landscape. The continuousness of your endeavours will fashion a new form from the rock – you hone your tools (breath, meditation, conscious awareness, etc.) and sculpt a destiny. You are not carving an idol and you are not confined to the rock – you are the weather as much as the rock. Mindfulness is a means as much as it is an end.

Action
Experience a rock

Go find a rock – up a hill, on a mountain, at the seashore – not a stone, a rock. One you can sit on, lie back upon, feel the solidness beneath your body, rub the texture of it with your hands. Millions of years in the making – the continuity of eternal reality is here. Touch it, feel it. Sit or lie on the rock and follow your breath – this is a Bodhi place. The whole earth is a Bodhi place. Inhale and exhale the eternal reality. You are as solid as this rock and as free as the weather that shaped it. Inhale and exhale and know that you are the eternal reality.

Foillsightear gach nidh le h-aimsir

By time is everything revealed

⤙

Be patient: all will be revealed. And in this context, all is almost revealed as we near the end of this book and explore the three last proverbs. These final three will stand to you and your continued journey beyond this reading experience, allowing you to go forward with faith, confidence and permission to seize the day.

As you progress on your journey – learning new skills and having insights – minutes, hours and days pass by, and life goes on. Before you know it, some distance has appeared between your novice approaches and your adept understanding of breath control, thought patterns and mindful action. The real life has been revealed, and all it took was time. There is even more to come. Fill those days mindfully and soon the lotus will open in every action of your life.

Good things come to those who wait, better things come to those who seek. Don't just sit (even in the lotus position) and wait – go and get it.

This proverb is not an excuse to do little. Instead, this seanfhocal reminds us that life fills our time and eventually life gives up its secrets and truths. You can sit under the Bodhi tree for a hundred years and not find enlightenment, and you can walk to the shops and feel filled with grace. Stop wasting time – get going, there is so much to come. The now of your next meditation or mindful practice is the now of the eternal coming and going. Now is eternal. Even in stillness you are dynamic, even in motion you are still you. The soul is indestructible. Time is immaterial – don't fret about it.

Action
Go outside

That's it – go outside now. Sun, snow, rain – no matter, just go outside and breathe the air, feel the temperature of the season upon your skin. This is now. This is your life. Are you living it? Enough reading, enough meditation for today – go do something. This is your time. Run around the block, climb a hill, swim a length, throw a Frisbee, jump the neighbour's hedge. Connecting with the outdoors strengthens the immune system, promotes better sleep, allays depression and fatigue, and energises the mind, body and soul.

Béarfaidh buicéad ar an uisce
A bucket will catch the water

～

This proverb speaks of faith – faith in the bucket – but it also speaks of purpose and the fulfilment of that purpose. We will be filled with grace, peace of mind, awareness, happiness, joy and gratitude. Sometimes being is enough. Inhabiting your body mindfully, meeting the world mindfully, living your life mindfully – that is the bucket filling. Just being in mindfulness, in awareness, is action. Just being still – in meditation, contemplation, connection with your breath or the breeze on your skin – is action.

If you cannot be – then become. Become mindful, self-aware, spiritually aware, compassionate, joyous, connected, real. Become it. Then you will be it.

Becoming mindful can be achieved by practice (of the spiritual exercises and of your intent to be so) and by patience (transforming without panic, rush, checklists or status updates). This beautiful, Zen-like seanfhocal lets us know the outcome is inevitable. If we become the vessel to be filled, we will be filled and it exquisitely informs us that nature will take its course. We need not fret – the bucket will catch the water, and you can have patience with it, which is a great luxury in this modern world. A reminder too to practise patience more often – to cultivate the serenity of self, to live in the now. If something takes time, that is more time to be. Say you choose to make a change and paint a room. If the undercoat is dry straight away then it only necessitates the next coat of paint – where is the space between to enjoy the gradual transition, to notice and experience the process of the change? We don't have to rush every move and action. We will get there, and can enjoy or at least fully partake of the journey. It is OK to have a cup of tea between coats of paint and admire your work thus far. The bucket will not lose its capacity to catch water between showers and dry spells. The bucket lives its full potential as a catcher of water constantly, in every second. Just as with every breath you are alive, be that up the step ladder or slurping tea.

As this proverb speaks of patience, it is good to note that while patience is a virtue so also can it be effortless – the bucket will catch the water. It is not only fit for purpose, but conforms to the laws of physics and the laws of nature – and it will gather by being what it is. Be what you want to be but be who you are – not what you think you are, or have been told you are, but what you *are* – radiant and unfolding love.

Action
Let the bucket fill

Place a bucket, basin or cup outside on a rainy day and let it be – let it catch the rain and fill to the measure that the rain gives. Later, use that water to wash your hair or feet – take the reward of the fluid and be fluid with it but always celebrate it by giving it an extra use. Wash mindfully; feel the lather, feel the rinse, contemplate the sensations of cleansing.

Is iomaí lá sa chill orainn

We are in the churchyard/grave many a day

—◆—

I am not going to pontificate much further, and this is the most appropriate end to this book. This final seanfhocal reminds us that we spend a long time dead – so live now while life fills you. Afterlife or reincarnation matters not – live this life.

The journey of this book, the time taken to read it and to put it into practice has brought you closer to life – to living well. Don't waste it. Journey on. Live well. Live now.

Action
Breathe now

That's it – just breathe. Inhale, exhale; feel every breath for a minute. Be fully in that minute, be in the now right now. Then go enjoy your day. This is the secret of life.

Further reading

While each entry in this book is a self-contained lesson, there are themes that run throughout – the physical effects of meditation, the power of practice to create change, finding and engaging peak experience, how altruism and personal action positively affect health, and so on. Below is a further reading section laid out by topic of interest. This will facilitate both further exploration of these topics and lay out the evidence-based research that was used to formulate some of the exercises and mindfulness tools contained in this book.

Physical effects of meditation

Berkovich-Ohana, A., Glicksohn, J. and Goldstein, A. (2012). Mindfulness-induced changes in gamma band activity – implications for the default mode network, self-reference and attention. *Clinical Neurophysiology*, 123(4), 700–10.

Brefczynski-Lewis, J. A., Lutz, A., Schaefer, H. S., Levinson D. B. and Davidson R. J. (2007). Neural correlates of attentional expertise in long-term meditation practitioners. *Proceedings of the National Academy of Science USA*, 104, 11483–8.

Chiesa, A. and Serretti, A. (2010). A systematic review of neurobiological and clinical features of mindfulness meditations. *Psychological Medicine*, 40, 1239–52.

Corbetta, M., Patel, G. and Shulman, G. L. (2008). The reorienting system of the human brain: From environment to theory of mind. *Neuron*, 58, 306–24.

Craig, A. D. (2002). How do you feel? Interoception: The sense of the physiological condition of the body. *Nature Reviews Neuroscience*, 3, 655–66.

Farb, N. A. S., Segal, Z. V., Mayberg, H., Bean, J., McKeon, D., Fatima, Z. and Anderson, A. K. (2007). Attending to the present: Mindfulness meditation reveals distinct neural modes of self-reference. *Social Cognitive and Affective Neuroscience*, 2, 313–22

Green, R., and Turner, G. (2010). Growing evidence for the influence of meditation on brain and behaviour. *Neuropsychological Rehabilitation*, 20, 306–11.

Hasenkamp, W. and Barsalou, L. W. (2012). Effects of meditation experience on functional connectivity of distributed brain networks. *Frontiers in Human Neuroscience*, 6(38) doi: 10.3389/fnhum.2012.00038. eCollection 2012.

Jha, A. P., Krompinger, J. and Baime, M. J. (2007). Mindfulness training modifies subsystems of attention. *Cognitive Affective and Behavioural Neuroscience*, 7, 109–19.

Kilpatrick, L. A., Suyenobu, B. Y., Smith, S. R., Bueller, J. A., Goodman, T., Creswell, J. D., Tillisch, K., Mayer, E. A. and Naliboff, B. D. (2011). Impact of mindfulness-based stress reduction training on intrinsic brain connectivity. *Neuroimage*, 56, 290–8.

Kozasa, E. H., Sato, J. R., Lacerda, S. S., Barreiros, M. A., Radvany, J., Russell, T. A., Sanches, L. G., Mello, L. E. and Amaro, E. Jr. (2012). Meditation training increases brain efficiency in an attention task. *Neuroimage*, 59, 745–9.

Lippelt, D. P., Hommel, B. and Colzato, L. S. (2014). Focused attention, open monitoring and loving kindness meditation: Effects on attention, conflict monitoring, and creativity – A review. *Frontiers in Psychology*, 5, 1083.

Lutz, A., Slagter, H. A., Dunne, J. D. and Davidson, R. J. (2008). Attention regulation and monitoring in meditation. *Trends in Cognitive Science*, 12, 163–9.

Lutz, A., Slagter, H. A., Rawlings, N. B., Francis, A. D., Greischar, L. L. and Davidson, R. J. (2009). Mental training enhances attentional stability: Neural and behavioral evidence. *Journal of Neuroscience*, 29, 13418–27.

Manna, A., Raffone, A., Perrucci, M., Nardo, D., Ferretti, A., Tartaro, A., Londei, A., Del Gratta, C., Belardinelli, M. O. and Romani, G. L. (2010). Neural correlates of focused attention and cognitive monitoring in meditation. *Brain Research Bulletin*, 82, 46–56.

Ospina, M., Bond, K., Karkhaneh, M., Tjosvold, L., Vanderneer, B., Liang, Y., Bialy, L., Hooton, N., Buscemi, N., Dryden, D. M. and Klassen, T. P. (2007). Meditation practices for health: State of the research. *Evidence Report/Technological Assessment*, 155, 1–263.

Pace, T. W., Negi, L. T., Adame, D. D., Cole, S. P., Sivilli, T. I., Brown, T. D., Issa, M. J. and Raison, C. L. (2009). Effect of compassion meditation on neuroendocrine, innate immune and behavioral responses to psychosocial stress. *Psychoneuroendocrinology*, 34, 87–98.

Rubia, K. (2009). The neurobiology of meditation and its clinical effectiveness in psychiatric disorders. *Biological Psychology*, 82, 1–11.

Xue, S., Tang, Y. Y. and Posner, M. I. (2011). Short-term meditation increases network efficiency of the anterior cingulate cortex. *NeuroReport*, 22, 570–74.

Yu, X., Fumoto, M., Nakatani, Y., Sekiyama, T., Kikuchi, H., Seki, Y., Sato-Suzuk,i I. and Arita, H. (2011). Activation of the anterior prefrontal cortex and serotonergic system is associated with improvements in mood and EEG changes induced by Zen meditation practice in novices. *International Journal of Psychophysiology*, 80, 103–11.

Zeidan, F., Johnson, S. K., Diamond, B. J., David, Z. and Goolkasian, P. (2010). Mindfulness meditation improves cognition: Evidence of brief mental training. *Consciousness and Cognition*, 19, 597–605.

The effects of gratitude

Algoe, S. B., Haidt, J. and Gable, S. L. (2008). Beyond reciprocity: Gratitude and relationships in everyday life. *Emotion*, 8, 425–9.

Bono, G., Emmons, R. A., and McCullough, M. E. (2004). Gratitude in practice and the practice of gratitude. In P. A. Linley and S. Joseph, eds, *Positive Psychology in Practice*. New Jersey: John Wiley and Sons. pp. 464–81.

Emmons, R. A. (2007). *Thanks! How the new science of gratitude can make you happier*. New York: Houghton-Mifflin.

Emmons, R. A. and Crumpler, C. A. (2000). Gratitude as a human strength: Appraising the evidence. *Journal of Social and Clinical Psychology*, 19, 56–69.

Emmons, R. A. and McCullough, M. E., eds (2004). *The Psychology of Gratitude*. New York: Oxford University Press.

Emmons, R. A. and Stern, R. (2013). Gratitude as a psychotherapeutic intervention. *Journal of Clinical Psychology*, 69(8), 846–55.

Fredrickson, B. L. and Branigan, C. (2005). Positive emotions broaden the scope of attention and thought-action repertoires. *Cognition and Emotion*, 19, 313–32.

McCullough, M. E., Emmons, R. A. and Tsang, J. A. (2002). The grateful disposition: A conceptual and empirical topography. *Journal of Personality and Social Psychology*, 82, 112–27.

Nowak, M. and Roch, S. (2006). Upstream reciprocity and the evolution of gratitude. *Proceedings of the Royal Society of London, Series B: Biological Sciences*, 274, 605–9.

Watkins, P. C., Woodward, K., Stone, T. and Kolts, R. L. (2003). Gratitude and happiness: Development of a measure of gratitude, and relationships with subjective wellbeing. *Social Behavior and Personality*, 31, 431–51.

Wood, A. M., Joseph, S. and Linley, P. A. (2007). Coping style as a psychological resource of grateful people. *Journal of Social and Clinical Psychology*, 26, 1108–25.

Wood, A. M., Joseph, S. and Linley, P. A. (2007). Gratitude: The parent of all virtues. *The Psychologist*, 20, 18–21.

Wood, A. M., Joseph, S. and Maltby, J. (2008). Gratitude uniquely predicts satisfaction with life: Incremental validity above the domains and facets of the five factor model. *Personality and Individual Differences*, 45, 49–54.

Wood, A. M., Maltby, J., Gillett, R., Linley, P. A. and Joseph, S. (2008). The role of gratitude in the development of social support, stress, and depression: Two longitudinal studies. *Journal of Research in Personality*, 42, 854–71.

Peak experience

Maslow, A. H. (1962). *Toward a Psychology of Being*. Princeton, NJ: Van Nostrand.

Maslow, A. H. (1964). *Religions, Values, and Peak Experiences.* London: Penguin Books.

Privette, G. (2001). Defining moments of self-actualization: Peak performance and peak experience. In K. J. Schneider, J. F. T. Bugental, and J. F. Pierson, eds, *The Handbook of Humanistic Psychology.* pp. 161–80.

Wilson, C. (2009). *Super Consciousness: The Quest for the Peak Experience.* London: Watkins.

The power of practice

Charness, N., Feltovich, P. J., Hoffman, R. R. and Ericsson, K. A., eds (2006). *The Cambridge Handbook of Expertise and Expert Performance.* Cambridge: University Press.

Gladwell, M. (2008). *Outliers: The story of success.* Boston: Little, Brown and Company.

Colvin, G. (2010). *Talent is Overrated: What really separates world-class performers from everybody else.* London: Portfolio.

The power of forgiveness

Berlant, L. G., ed. (2004). *Compassion: The culture and politics of an emotion*. New York: Routledge.

Lawler, K. A., Younger, J. W., Piferi, R. L., Jobe, R. L., Edmondson, K. A. and Jones, W. H. (2005) The unique effects of forgiveness on health: An exploration of pathways. *Journal of Behavioral Medicine*, 28(2), 157–67.

McCullough, M. E. (2000). Forgiveness as human strength (theory, measurement, and links to well-being). *Journal of Social and Clinical Psychology*, 19, 43–55.

Toussaint, L. L., Owen, A. D. and Cheadle, A. (2012). Forgive to live: Forgiveness, health, and longevity. *Journal of Behavioral Medicine*, 35(4), 375–86.

van Oyen Witvliet, C., Ludwig, T. E. and Vander Laan, K. L. (2001). Granting forgiveness or harboring grudges: implications for emotion, physiology, and health. *Psychological Science*, 12, 117–23.

Worthington, E. L., ed. (2005). *Handbook of Forgiveness*. New York: Brunner-Routledge.

Happiness and wellbeing studies

Anderson, N. B. (2003). *Emotional Longevity: What really determines how long you live*. New York: Viking.

Diener, E. (1984). Subjective well-being. *Psychological Bulletin*, 95, 542–75.

Diener, E. and Biswas-Diener, R. (2008). *Happiness: Unlocking the mysteries of psychological wealth*. Oxford: Blackwell.

Diener, E. and Chan, M. Y. (2011). Happy people live longer: Subjective well-being contributes to health and longevity. *Applied Psychology: Health and Well-Being*, 3, 1–43.

Edwards, J. R. and Cooper, C. L. (1988). The impacts of positive psychological states on physical health: Review and theoretical framework. *Social Science and Medicine*, 27, 1447–59.

Kim, E. S., Park, N., Sun, J. K., Smith, J. and Peterson, C. (2014). Life satisfaction and frequency of doctor visits. *Psychosomatic Medicine*, 76(1), 86–93.

Lamers, S. M. A., Bolier, L., Westerhof, G. J., Smit, F. and Bohlmeijer, E. T. (2012). The impact of emotional well-being on long-term recovery and survival in physical illness: A meta-analysis. *Journal of Behavioral Medicine*, 35(5), 538–47.

Layard, R. (2005). *Happiness: Lessons from a new science*. London: Allen Lane.

Sternberg, E. M. (2001). *The Balance Within: The science connecting health and emotions*. New York: Freeman.

Altruism and health

Baumeister, R. F. and Leary, M. R. (1995). The need to belong: Desire for interpersonal attachments as a fundamental human motivation. *APA Psychological Bulletin*, 117(3), 497–529.

Brown, S., Brown, R. M. and Preston, S. (2011). A neuroscience model of caregiving motivation. In S. Brown, R. M. Brown and L. Penner, eds, *Moving Beyond Self Interest: Perspectives from evolutionary biology, neuroscience, and the social sciences*. New York: Oxford University Press.

Brown, S. L., Nesse, R. M., Vinokur, A. D. and Smith, D. M. (2003). Providing social support may be more beneficial than receiving it: Results from a prospective study of mortality. *Psychological Science*, 14(4), 320–7.

Brown, S. L., Smith, D. M., Schulz, R., Kabeto, M. U., Ubel, P. A., Poulin, M., Yi, J., Kim, C. and Langa, K. M. (2009). Caregiving behavior is associated with decreased mortality risk. *Psychological Science* 20(4), 488–94.

Dunn, E. W., Aknin, L. B. and Norton, M. I. (2008). Spending money on others promotes happiness. *Science*, 319(5870), 1687–8

House, J., Landis, K. and Umberson, D. (1988). Social relationships and health. *Science*, 241(4865), 540–5.

Jamal, A. and McKinnon, H. (2010). *The Power of Giving: How giving back enriches us all*. New York: TarcherPerigee.

Liang, J., Krause, N. M. and Bennett, J. M. (2001). Social exchange and well-being: Is giving better than receiving? *Psychology and Aging*, 16(3), 511–23.

Lu, L. (1997). Social support, reciprocity, and well-being. *Journal of Social Psychology*, 137(5), 618–28.

Lu, L. and Argyle, M. (1992). Receiving and giving support: Effects on relationships and wellbeing. *Counselling Psychology Quarterly*, 5(2), 123–33.

Moll, J., Krueger, F., Zahn, R., Pardini, M., de Oliveira-Souza, R. and Grafman, J. (2006). Human fronto-mesolimbic networks guide decisions about charitable donation. *Proceedings of the National Academy of Science USA*, 103(42), 15623–8.

Post, S., ed. (2007). *Altruism and Health*. New York: Oxford University Press.

Poulin, M. J., Brown, S. L., Dillard, A. J. and Smith, D. M. (2013). Giving to others and the association between stress and mortality. *American Journal of Public Health*, 103(9), 1649–55.

Rodrigues, S. M., Saslow, L. R., Garcia, N., John, O. P. and Keltner, D. (2009). Oxytocin receptor genetic variation relates to empathy and stress reactivity in humans. *Proceedings of the National Academy of Science USA*, 106(50), 21437–41.

Ryan, M. J. (2000). *The Giving Heart: Unlocking the transformative power of generosity in your life.* Newburyport: Conari Press.

Schwartz, C., Meisenhelder, J. B., Ma, Y. and Reed, G. (2003). Altruistic social interest behaviours are associated with better mental health. *Psychosomatic Medicine*, 65(5),778–85.

Schwartz, C. and Sendor, R. M. (1999). Helping others helps oneself: Response shift effects in peer support. *Social Science and Medicine*, 48(11), 1563–75.

Yinon, Y. and Landau, M. O. (1987). On the reinforcing value of helping behavior in a positive mood. *Motivation and Emotion*, 11(1), 83–93.

List of proverbs